FIRST STEPS in WINEMAKING

FIRST STEPS in WINEMAKING

C.J.J.Berry

An Amateur Winemaker Book

Special Interest Model Books Ltd.
P.O. Box 327
Poole
Dorset
BH15 2RG

First published by Amateur Winemaker
Eighth edition 1987
Reprinted 1988, 1989, 1990, 1991, 1992, 1993 (twice), 1994, 1995 (twice)
Ninth edition 1996, reprinted 1997, 1999

This edition published by Special Interest Model Books Ltd. 2002

Reprinted 2003, 2004, 2005, 2006

www.specialinterestmodelbooks.co.uk

ISBN 1-85486-139-5
ISBN-13 978-185486-137-5

Printed and bound in Great Britain by Biddles Ltd. www.biddles.co.uk

About this book

This little book started life as a collection of recipes, reliable recipes which had appeared in the monthly magazine, *The Amateur Winemaker*. First published in January 1960, it was an instant and phenomenal success, so much so that over 3 million copies have been sold, and it has become internationally recognised as the best 'rapid course' in winemaking available to the beginner.

It is very different now from the original small book, of course, for as new developments have occurred in winemaking and fresh knowledge has been available it has been continually updated and amended in the course of some 130 printings, and this latest version is again a much improved book, including new material and photographs.

Britain has now gone metric, and I was tempted to change completely to that system of measurement, but I know that winemakers are still fighting a rearguard action and that there are thousands of them who still prefer the old imperial measures. And since the most popular single vessel still in use is the 'one-gallon jar' that forms the basis of so much of our winemaking practice – and seems likely to continue to do so – I give quantities in both systems, metric and imperial. To do this, and to be able to correlate the two, I have had necessarily to talk about '4.5 litres' (i.e. 1 gallon) rather than 5 litres, or the book would become unduly confusing. For the same reason I have rounded off metric quantities to the nearest sensible level, rather than always giving the precise equivalent of the imperial. Again, for the sake of simplicity, I have quoted '1-gallon' quantities for our American friends but I am quite well aware that their gallon is so small – only four-fifths of ours – that they are accustomed to make at least three to five gallons at a time. The answer is simple; they should just multiply the quantities given (except perhaps the yeast) by the number of gallons they intend to make.

Many of the recipes have been slightly adjusted from their original form to conform to modern practice, but they are still mainly arranged in the months of their making, so that you can pursue your winemaking all the year round with this veritable winemaker's almanac.

Those who have just fallen under the spell of this fascinating hobby of ours will also want to know more of its technicalities, so this book includes a wealth of practical tips and certain factual information that any winemaker would find useful. In particular, the hydrometer, ignored in many books on winemaking, is dealt with simply but adequately . . . you will find this small book a mine of useful information. Above all, I have tried to convey the information you will need simply and clearly, without any of the mystique or jargon which to my mind spoils so many books on the subject.

As your winemaking experience grows there is no doubt that you will wish to extend your experiments to making wines like those of commerce, making your own liqueurs, brewing beer or making mead.

I hope you will enjoy this book as much as I enjoyed writing it . . . best wishes for successful winemaking!

The author looks up a reference in his library of commercial and country wine books for a friend.

A fascinating craft

If you are toying with the idea of trying your hand at winemaking, delay no longer. Go right ahead! By doing so you will be joining the thousands of people who, in recent years, have discovered this intriguing and rewarding hobby. It is, indeed, a pastime which truly 'brings its own rewards', for there can be few pleasures to equal that of being able to offer friends, and enjoy with them, a glass of one's own wine.

After World War II, when sugar was rationed and there was little opportunity to follow the hobby, there was an astonishing growth in home winemaking, and nowadays it still attracts the interest of thousands, wine and beer kits are on sale in many large stores, every town has its home brew shop, and in peak years the 'industry' was reputed to have turned over £65 to £75 million pounds annually, the bulk of it on wine and beer kits. Many people, however, are still happiest making 'country wines', i.e. wines from garden or hedgerow fruits and vegetables, and thanks to the advancement of winemaking knowledge there is now no reason why you should have difficulty in producing delicious wines in your own home at a fraction of the cost of equivalent quality commercial wines.

This phenomenal interest in winemaking parallels – or is a contributory cause of? – the enormous increase in the consumption of commercial wines in the last 30 years. Certainly we are all drinking more wine, and that is an excellent reason for making your own and having an unlimited supply!

In this country there is absolutely no restriction upon how much wine you make as long as it is entirely for your own consumption, but since no duty has been paid upon it *not a drop must be sold*, or you will be in trouble with the law. This prohibition, it should be noted, may well be held to extend to 'cheese and wine' parties using home-made wine if a charge is made for admission, and to the raffling of home-made wines, even for a good cause.

Above all, note that distilling is both dangerous, in that alcohols which are not safely potable may be produced, and illegal, carrying very heavy penalties. The same is true of the separation of alcohol by freezing; the offence is in the separation of alcohol by distillation 'or any other means.' Do not try either process: the risks, both physical and legal, make them just not worth the candle.

What you will need

Do not buy a lot of expensive equipment at the outset, it is better to *start* making wine with what you have – you probably already have in your kitchen some of the essentials – and then acquire the rest by stages as the necessity arises.

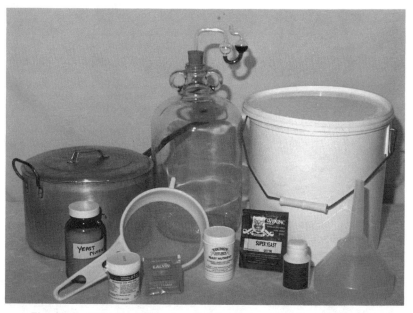

First kit for 'First Steps'! Saucepan, 2 gallon bucket and siphon tube, 1 gallon jar with bung and fermentation lock, funnel, strainer, yeast, nutrient and citric acid.

You may decide to start out with a beginner's kit, which can be purchased in most large stores and will set you on the road to making your first gallon, but let us assume that you are going to make 'country wines'. For that you will undoubtedly need some kind of boiler, and if you can lay your hands on one that will hold three to five gallons it will prove ideal. Failing that, you can 'make do' with a one-gallon or one-and-a-half-gallon saucepan.

Ideal fermenting bin.

Avoid containers and utensils of iron, brass and copper, which may be affected by acids and impart hazes and flavours to your wine; use only boilers of aluminium, stainless steel or sound, unchipped, enamel ware.

You will also need a large vessel in which to do your soaking, or mashing, and one of three to five gallons is ideal. It is preferable to have one in a high-density synthetic material such as polypropylene (the harder and whiter the material the better) and since such brew-bins are nowadays so readily available in winemaking shops there is really no excuse for using plastic dustbins or similar coloured containers which are not intended for food and may well contain toxic colourants. Far better to invest in a proper brew-bin – it will last you several years. You probably already have a white polythene bucket, and will find this extremely useful for small quantities.

Also obtain several one-gallon jars (4.5 litres) for fermenting – those with 'ear' handles (demijohns) are the most popular – and some rubber bungs and corks to fit. One point: these jars can vary greatly in size

An 11-pint saucepan like this one makes a good first boiler.

and it is as well to employ a pint measure to discover exactly how much yours holds. You can also use food-grade plastic bottles or cubes of this size. But *try* always to stick to glass – it is always safer and can convey no flavour. On no account omit to buy or make as many fermentation traps (see separate chapter) as you are likely to need, for they are indeed the winemaker's best friend.

You will also find it useful to collect 1-litre and half-gallon bottles (Winchesters, free from your chemist) and a supply of white wine bottles – NOT squash or sauce bottles, *please!* – and corks or stoppers to fit. It is false economy to use old corks, which may infect your wine; always use new corks, and soak them in a sterilising solution before insertion. Alternatively, buy some of the new plastic stoppers which can be used over and over again, after sterilising by boiling water.

You will also need some small packets of chemicals such as citric acid, pectolytic enzyme, tannin, yeast nutrient, a good general purpose wine yeast and lastly, a metre length of clear plastic siphon tube, for racking your wines.

A collection of funnels and measures for various jobs is useful.

This list may sound formidable, but if you buy just the 'First kit' illustrated on page 9, the total cost is likely to be in the region of only £10 (1995 prices).

Refinements

These are the bare essentials, but undoubtedly as you progress in wine-making you will add other pieces of desirable equipment – a thermometer, a hydrometer for calculating the strength of your wine, glass tubing for taking samples, small funnels, casks, stone jars, tie-on labels for jars and stick-on labels for bottles, a corking device, a cork borer, filtering apparatus, a bottle cleaning brush, and perhaps a small press or one of the quite inexpensive juice extractors now obtainable which can do so very much to remove the 'cookery' from winemaking and make it that more pleasurable. You may even go to the length of wanting to be *entirely* sure of accuracy, so much so that you will need some acid measuring equipment. And as you progress you will want to make wine in larger quantities, for which you will need larger utensils. More of this later, but there is no need to bother about all this at the outset. That is the beauty of winemaking – you can tackle it as you please, either in comparatively simple fashion with the help of recipes, or by going the whole hog and delving more fully into its scientific side, making up country wines to suit your taste in the light of your experience.

Wine vocabulary

Acidity   One of the most important characteristics of wine: obtaining the correct acidity is all-important.

Acetification   Turning to vinegar.

Aerobic fermentation   A fermentation conducted in the presence of air. Usually the first part of the fermentation process.

Alcohol   In wine, ethyl alcohol.

Ammonium phosphate   A popular yeast nutrient.

Ammonium sulphate   A popular yeast nutrient.

Anaerobic fermentation   A fermentation from which air is excluded; the second part of the fermentation process.

13

Aperitif   A wine taken before a meal to induce good appetite.

Aroma   The smell of a young wine.

Bentonite   A diatomaceous earth or clay used as a wine fining or clarifier.

Body   The fullness of a wine.

Bouquet   The smell of a mature wine.

Campden tablets   Useful in winemaking for various sterilisation or purification purposes. They supply sulphur dioxide in convenient form.

Carbon dioxide   The colourless, odourless gas given off by a fermenting liquor.

Concentrate   The juice of white or red wine grapes concentrated and sold in tins or packs.

Country wines   Wines made from fruit or ingredients other than the grape.

Demi john   Another name for a 1-gallon jar.

Dessert wines   Strong, full-bodied and full-flavoured wines drunk at the end of a meal with the dessert course.

Dry   A wine is said to be dry when all the sugar in it has been used up by the fermentation; it is also said to have 'fermented right out'.

Enzyme   Protein catalysts used in winemaking and brewing to promote structural breakdown or changes in ingredients. Pectin-destroying enzymes are particularly useful in preventing jellification or cloudiness in fruit wines.

Ex-wine five   A plastic 5-gallon cube previously used for draught sherry or commercial wines or fruit juices (not now easily obtainable).

Fermenting (or working)   The process brought about by yeast acting upon sugar to produce alcohol and carbon dioxide.

Fermentation trap (or airlock)   A little gadget used to protect the fermentation from infection by the vinegar fly. Also called a 'bubbler'.

Filtration   Clarifying a wine by the use of a filter, using powders, papers, or pads.

Final gravity   The specific gravity when fermentation has finished.

Fining   Removing suspended solids from a cloudy wine by adding wine finings.

Flogger   A wooden tool for banging corks home, now replaced by corking guns.

Fortification   Increasing the strength of wine beyond that possible by natural fermentation by adding spirit.

Gravity   An abbreviation of 'specific gravity', a scale used to measure the density of a liquid or, in winemaking usage, its sugar content.

Hydrometer   An instrument for measuring the weight (or sugar content) of a liquid.

Hydrometer jar   The jar in which a hydrometer is floated for a reading to be taken.

Initial gravity   The specific gravity at the outset of fermentation.

Lees   The deposit of yeast and solids formed during fermentation.

Magnesium sulphate (Epsom salts)   A yeast nutrient.

Malo-lactic fermentation   See p. 70.

Metabisulphite   Widely-used chemical for sterilisation or preservation of wines. See Potassium and Sodium metabisulphite.

Must   The pulp or combination of basic ingredients from which a wine is made.

Nutrient   Nitrogenous matter added to the liquor to boost the action of the yeast; yeast food.

Oxidation   When wine darkens and goes brown on contact with air.

Pectic enzyme   A preparation used to destroy the pectin, or clouding agent, in a wine or must.

Pectin   A substance which makes jams 'set' – and causes hazes in fruit wines.

Polypin   (see ex-wine five).

Potassium metabisulphite   A sterilising chemical.

Potassium phosphate   A yeast nutrient.

Proof   An obsolete system of expressing the alcohol strength of a drink. 100° proof spirit contained 57.1% alcohol. Now replaced by a simple % alcohol by volume, so that a bottle of spirit that was 70° proof is now

15

labelled as 40% abv. The USA still has a 'proof' measurement, which is 50% abv.

Racking   Siphoning the wine off the lees to clear and stabilise it.

Social wines   Wines meant to be drunk 'socially' (e.g. whilst watching the 'telly'!) and not necessarily with food. Not usually completely dry.

Sodium metabisulphite   As Potassium metabisulphite.

Specific gravity   See Gravity.

Stable   A wine is said to be stable when there is no danger of further fermentation.

Sticking   When fermentation stops prematurely, before enough sugar has been converted.

Stopper   A cork or polythene bottle closure with a projecting cap.

Straining   Removing solids after a pulp fermentation.

Strength   This is usually quoted as per cent alcohol by volume (abv), i.e. that many parts in a hundred are alcohol.

Tannin   The substance which lends wine its astringency and gives it keeping qualities.

Titration   A method of determining acidity.

Ullage   The air space between the surface of the wine and the bottom of the cork or bung.

Vinegar   Wine which has 'gone wrong'.

Vitamin B1   A useful yeast nutrient.

Yeast   The *real* winemaker!

Cleanliness and sterility

Complete cleanliness is most important to the winemaker: all vessels, bottles and equipment must be not only visually clean but chemically clean. Airborne yeasts and vinegar and other bacteria can only be kept at bay by constant vigilance.

It is perhaps important to distinguish between cleanliness and sterility.

Cleaning

For the simple cleaning of bottles, casks or apparatus which have heavily soiled surfaces ordinary *cleaning solutions* can be used, either

Soda   125 g (4 oz) washing soda in 5 litres (1 gallon) of water,

OR

Hypochlorite   25 g (1 fl oz) domestic bleach in 5 litres (1 gallon) water. Rinse thoroughly afterwards.

Sterilising

Means what it says, not only cleaning, but killing any bacteria present as well.

Modern developments in brewery cleaning chemicals have resulted in the production of multi-action products such as Chempro, V.W.P. or Hambleton Bard Supreme, and I personally now use one of these – Chempro – because it has been formulated to *clean and sterilise in one operation.*

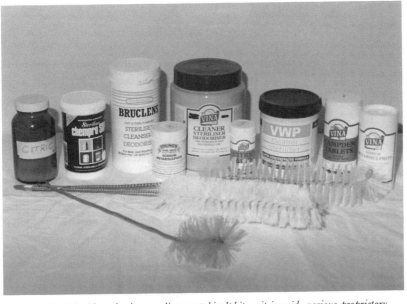

Useful aids to hygiene: sodium metabisulphite, citric acid, various proprietary cleaners/sterilisers and bottle brushes.

A short soaking swiftly removes and rinses away any surface dirt and bacteria, leaving bottles and jars sparkling clean and completely sterile, with virtually no effort. This so greatly simplifies the job that I would advise you to adopt this method right from the start.

Sulphite

It is slightly less expensive, of course, to make up your own sterilant, and for this you can use sulphite, sodium or potassium metabisulphite, sold either as Campden tablets (ordinary fruit preserving tablets) or as crystals. One Campden tablet contains 7 grains, 0.44 g, or 50 ppm in 1 gallon.

Make up a sterilising solution by dissolving 6 tablets and 10 g (two level teaspoons) of citric acid in 500 ml (1 pint) of water, and use it to sterilise all your jars, bottles and equipment by rinsing them with it. Note that it must be kept in a tightly stoppered bottle or it will deteriorate. And avoid inhaling the fumes, particularly if you are asthmatic.

A small quantity can be used to do many jars and bottles by pouring it from one to the other, corking, rolling, and shaking each one in turn so that all parts of the interior are moistened. Wipe round the neck of the bottle with cotton wool dipped in the solution.

Glass jars, carboys and bottles can safely be stored and kept sterile if half an inch of the solution is left in the bottom of each, and they are tightly corked.

Other uses of sulphite: it can also be used to suppress unwanted bacteria and 'wild' yeasts before a fermentation, and to stabilise a wine; thus:

To purify 'must' before fermentation	1 Campden tablet
On second racking (q.v.):	1 Campden tablet
To stabilise wine completely:	2 – 3 tablets
	all per gallon

To use crystals instead: for a 10 per cent solution, dissolve ¼ lb sodium metabisulphite in 1 pint of hot water (100 g in 500 ml) and dilute this to a final volume of 1 quart (1 litre) once all the crystals have been dissolved. One teaspoon (5 ml) of this stock solution equals 1 Campden tablet.

But remember! – Work in a well-ventilated room and avoid inhaling the fumes: they can cause irritation to the eyes, nose and throat.

18

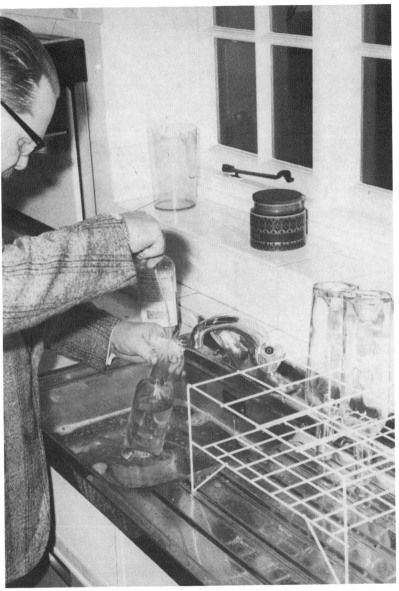

Bottles must be sterile and sparkling clean. Chempro or Steraglass are a great help.

With one of the popular wine kits now on the market you can be 'in business' right away, particularly with one as complete as this.

Kits and concentrates

Perhaps you were first attracted to winemaking when someone gave you a 'kit' as a Christmas or birthday present? Or when you first saw wine kits or apparatus on sale in a chain store or in your local home brew shop? Thousands come to the hobby nowadays in this way.

Many firms have produced attractive kits with full instructions to enable a beginner to make his first gallon with ease. Some of the principal manufacturers and firms have now raised this to a high level of sophistication, and one can now buy kits for making delightful wines like recognisable commercial types – Hock, Burgundy, Sauternes, Sherry, etc. – although by EEC regulations they cannot now be advertised under such titles. It is only fair to say that the quality can vary greatly, according to whose kit you use, and how well you follow the instructions.

Specialist shops like Whitby Homebrew at Ellesmere Port can offer you a wide range of wine (and beer) kits and accessories.

The choice of kits has never been greater, with over 30 brands offering upwards of 500 different kits, ranging from light delicate table wines to powerful strong liqueur wines. The price range is equally wide ranging, from as low as around £3 to make 1 gallon (6 bottles), to £25 to make 5 gallons (30 bottles) of table wine. There are many variations in this range of prices, with kits varying from packs of dried fruits and flowers to gallon containers of concentrated grape juice, or juice and sugar syrup, that need no sugar adding by the winemaker.

Many top-quality kits employ grape concentrate, which has merely to be diluted and fermented. This of course is very near to the wine of commerce – the fermented juice of freshly pressed grapes – but made at a cost far below the price of wine bought in a shop.

A fairly recent innovation has been the introduction of grape juices derived from specific types of grape. As in the commercial wine world, these are known as varietal wines, and you can choose between, say, a Cabernet Sauvignon and a Merlot for a red wine, or a Chenin and a Chardonnay for a white wine.

There are also wine kits, however (notably those imported from Scandinavia for making express or 'three-week' wines) which are a blend of concentrated fruit juices other than grape – apple, gooseberry, cherry, elderberry etc, often supplemented by dried sloes, hawthorn berries and so on – and these are generally a little cheaper. These kits usually include a series of sachets containing yeast and nutrients, and materials for fining, clearing, and stabilising the wine after fermentation has ended.

Many people nowadays use just these kits, and bypass the laborious part of winemaking, the flavour extraction from fruits etc. They do produce wine at very reasonable prices. Naturally they cost more than country wines produced from raw materials harvested by the winemaker, but you can still make wine for about 60p a bottle (1995) upwards, for table wines of 10–12% alcohol by volume.

Within the last few years, kits have been developed that will produce liqueur wines purely by fermentation. They ferment to at least 20% alcohol by volume, just a few per cent below, say, a commercial Cherry Brandy. Most commercial liqueurs are in the 20–40% abv range, so these kits mark a huge step forward in home fermentations. The latest advance has been to produce 'spirit' wine kits, which also ferment to 20% abv or more, and are flavoured to make convincing imitations of commercial spirits at half-strength. These kits really do produce excellent substitutes for the real thing, often indistinguishable when blended with a mixer, the way that most spirits are drunk.

Despite the commercial vintners' cry that only grape juice could produce good wine, there has been a steady supply of apple juice for wine, kits for mead, dried fruits for winemaking, kits for peach and apricot wines. And now the wheel has turned full circle. Currently on the market are commercial kits, intended to duplicate the country wines the hobby started with – tea, parsnip, elderflower, beetroot, and so on. There has even been a pea-pod wine kit!

Using concentrate

Some kits using concentrate once tended to produce rather 'lifeless' wines, which I found were greatly improved by blending in a little fresh fruit juice of a compatible type.

Grape concentrate is perhaps even better used as an additive in fruit wine musts, to improve their vinosity. (This was the purpose of including ½ lb or 1 lb raisins – dried grapes – in old-time recipes.) Try substituting ¼ pint (140 ml) grape concentrate for ½ lb raisins, and include this much concentrate in every gallon of your wine; it effects a great improvement in flavour and is quite inexpensive. It is therefore a good idea to keep available both white and red varieties in your winery.

A quarter of a pint of concentrate can be used to replace 3 oz sugar in a recipe, unless it is more than usually concentrated, when less will be needed, of course.

Wine kits and grape concentrate certainly have their uses, not the least among them being the opportunity they give you of having a bulk of wine ready to drink quickly while your own country wines are maturing and reaching their full potential. A 5-gallon wine kit is a marvellous idea if you wish to throw a party; by planning six weeks or so ahead you can have unlimited wine!

Wine kits will at least quickly demonstrate that it is perfectly possible to make good, palatable wine at home.

But, since you are reading this book, you obviously wish to know more about the basic principles, and about the possibility of making equally good wines from fruits other than the grape.

What wine is

True wine is the product of the grape, we are often reminded, but any winemaker of experience will assure you that we have no cause to feel in any way ashamed of the wines which can be produced from kits or from our native fruits, berries and flowers. Many of these sound wines, robust or delicate according to character, dry or sweet according to one's taste, are truly wines in their own right, quite capable of standing comparison with many which can be obtained commercially. You may find this difficult to believe but, when you have produced what you *think* is a good country wine, compare it with a commercial wine of similar type, and we guarantee you will be pleasantly surprised.

Once you understand the basic principles it is by no means difficult to make wine at home. True, the more you make, the more discerning and critical your palate will become, and the more you will find yourself seeking to capture those elusive qualities which go to make a great wine. Even the complete beginner can, by following a recipe, produce a sound and satisfying wine – often without knowing how or why! It is, however, infinitely better to understand the principles of the craft.

Our wines have four main ingredients initially: (1) Yeast, (2) Sugar, (3) Flavour and (4) Water. There are others which play their parts – notably acids, tannin and substances which nourish the yeast – but for simplicity's sake we will ignore them for the moment, and deal with them later. Time, the time required for maturation, also plays an important part.

Of these main ingredients undoubtedly the most important is YEAST. Yeast is a minute living organism which brings about fermentation, and if the fermentation is to be successful the yeast must be given ideal conditions in which to work. Those conditions are found in a sugary, slightly acid solution such as fruit juicce, when certain other yeast nutrients are present and when the temperature is favourable, say 18 – 24°C (65 – 75°F).

Fermentation

The alcohol which we seek as an ingredient of our wine is a by-product of the yeast's process of self-reproduction.

When the yeast is put into a sugary solution, it begins to multiply vigorously, and in the complex chemical processes which ensue, the sugar is converted roughly half to alcohol by weight and half to carbon dioxide – the bubbles in your beer, wine, cider or champagne.

It is an encouraging thought that for every bubble you see in your wine there is an equal weight of alcohol! The fermentation will be in two stages, but there is no distinct dividing line. The first, the aerobic ('with air') fermentation, will be comparatively vigorous, perhaps with some froth, but may last only five or six days. The wine will then settle down to the secondary, anaerobic ('without air') ferment, which will be much quieter and which towards the end may be barely discernible. This may last two, three, or four months, or even longer.

Temperature plays an important part. Above 38°C (100°F) the yeast will certainly be killed; at too low a temperature it will ferment only very slowly, if at all. A fermentation should be started off at about 21°C (70°F), the secondary fermentation should be at about 16°C (65°F), and the finished wine should be stored at 10°C to 13°C (50–55°F). So the temperatures are easy to remember – 20°, 15°, 10°C (or 70°, 60°, 50°F). A slow quiet fermentation usually produces better wine than a fast, over-vigorous and short one, and there is no need to be fussy within 2°C.

During the secondary fermentation it is wise to employ a device called a fermentation trap, or airlock, which both cuts off the air supply to the yeast and protects your wine from bacterial infection, of which more later.

As the fermentation proceeds, so the alcohol content increases, until finally it reaches a concentration (usually about 15–16 per cent alcohol by volume) which is such as to inhibit the yeast, preventing any further activity. Any sugar still left in the wine then remains only as a sweetening agent. Once the fermentation is finished the wine will not normally become any stronger no matter how long it is kept, although it will undoubtedly mellow with maturity. So discount all the stories you hear on the lines '. . . and this wine was 40 years old; it had become as strong as whisky!'

'Ware vinegar!

The worst possible mishap which can befall a winemaker is to have his wine at one stage or another turn to vinegar (from the French *vinaigre*: sour wine), which it can quite easily do if vinegar bacteria are allowed access to it. These bacteria are, like yeasts, present everywhere about us, but are sometimes introduced to the wine by infected equipment, or by that obnoxious carrier the fruit, or vinegar, fly (*Drosophila melanogaster*). This tiny fly, which appears as if by magic around any fermenting liquor or fruit, is the winemaker's biggest enemy; it must at all costs be kept from your wine. If it gains access to it the liquor, instead of turning to alcohol, may turn to vinegar, and you will have the sad task of pouring it down the drain or using it for cooking, for it will be quite irreclaimable.

The wine can be attacked by bacteria, either airborne or carried by the fly, at any stage, and that is why you *must* cover the first ferment closely with a thick cloth, plastic sheet, or lid. The principal danger, however, occurs not so much then, when the ferment is vigorous and largely protected by the carbon dioxide gas being given off, as during the slow, quiet secondary fermentation.

The fermentation trap

It is then that you need to use a fermentation trap, or airlock, to protect the ferment; it will let gas pressure escape but admit no air.

The trap, incidentally, has a secondary purpose. The yeast, for the reproductive process which it first employs, needs oxygen.

When, by means of the fermentation trap, we cut off its air supply, we force it to turn to a secondary method of self-reproduction which it can use without oxygen, and which is appreciably more productive of alcohol. Of this, naturally, we are wholly in favour!

The airlock is also a valuable indicator as to when fermentation is finished.

It is a simple device, and we illustrate the most popular patterns – the U-type with two bulbs and the cup type. Both are now made in plastic; the former can still be bought in its glass form. Whichever sort you use, it is inserted in the bung or cork of the fermenting vessels so as to be an airtight fit (this is important, or the lock will not work), and a good tip is to use rubber bungs rather than corks to ensure that there is no leakage. It is advisable to grease a glass trap's stem lightly and hold it in a thick

Popular patterns of fermentation lock.

cloth when pushing it home, to avoid the risk of breakage and a hand badly cut by jagged glass. The bottom of the stem must be above the level of the fermenting liquor; a half to three-quarters of an inch is normally sufficient, as long as the liquor is not frothing so vigorously as to force it out through the trap.

The U-bend of the trap is then filled with water, to the bottom of the bulbs, and in the water is dissolved one-eighth of a Campden tablet. Thus, even if a vinegar fly gets into the water and meets an untimely end, your wine will be safe, whereas if you have plain water in your trap it may become infected with the bacteria from the dead fly. In that case, since the inner end of the water is in aerial contact with your wine, it is still possible for your wine to be infected. So always use this small quantity of sulphite in the bend of your traps, and renew it every month or so. Alternatively, use glycerine of borax in the trap, which is less volatile and will not deteriorate. Yet another method is to use plain water, but to plug the top of the trap with a tiny tuft of cotton wool to deny dust and flies access.

As the wine ferments, it gives off carbon dioxide, which quickly builds up a pressure within the fermentation jar or bottle, and then pushes its way through the solution in a U-type trap with quite a musical 'blup... blup...blup'. This, you will find, is quite fascinating to watch. As the ferment proceeds, the bubbles will pass ever more slowly until finally the solution in the trap remains poised and no more gas passes. It is then a good idea to move the jar into a warm room for five or six days to see if any further activity develops. If not, it can be assumed that the fermentation has finished ... but make sure that your cork or bung is still airtight and that gas is not escaping through it or from its junction with the tube of the trap, or naturally the trap will not work.

The cup type of lock has become increasingly popular in recent years and is available in several patterns. Many like this type of lock because it is not so fragile as the glass bubbler, but it is not so satisfying to watch or listen to! It consists of a cup into which the tube from the fermentation jar rises, and inverted over the end of the tube is another, smaller-diameter, cup. Sulphite solution is poured into the trap and when gas is given off by the ferment it lifts the inner cup up and down to escape beneath its rim, through the solution. As with the glass bubbler, you need to inspect the trap from time to time to make sure that it still contains plenty of solution, and that too much has not evaporated.

When wine is maturing in store in the demijohn, it is easy to overlook an airlock that has dried out, and potentially admitting bacteria and wild yeasts that can spoil your precious wine. This can be avoided by using a safety-valve, one fitted with a piece of rubber tubing that will keep air out, but allow excess internal pressure (such as from a refermentation in a sweet wine) to escape safely – like a bicycle tyre valve in reverse.

Making your own

There are several other patterns of airlock on the market and you will eventually decide for yourself which you prefer, and may well even make your own. A plastic tube leading down into an aspirin bottle or yeast phial containing sulphite solution and secured to the fermenting vessel with sticky tape will answer quite well as long as you remember to remove the phial before uncorking the jar. If you do not, the sulphite solution will be siphoned back into your wine as you withdraw the cork and thus reduce the pressure inside the fermenting bottle. It should be noted that this minor disaster can also happen if the pressure inside the fermenting vessel happens to drop below that of the surrounding atmosphere; the sulphite in the trap will be sucked into the wine, which is bad for the wine and worse for the temper.

Another simple idea is to use an ordinary rubber balloon, stretching it over the neck of the jar. The pressure of the gas will inflate the balloon, and when inflation ceases the ferment is finished. For wide-necked jars or crocks one can use a sheet of polythene, secured with a stout rubber band. This, too, will be bulged out by the pressure of the gas which will escape from beneath the band.

These ideas are quite useful in the initial stages of fermentation, when the must often tends to foam quite vigorously, and can froth out through an airlock and down the side of the jar, making an awful mess. True, it is easily cleaned up and the rinsed airlock replaced, but it is even simpler to take the precaution of using a plug of cotton wool or a piece of polythene plus an elastic band, which can be thrown away, instead of an airlock. It also helps to stand the jar on a tray, to collect any yeasty overflow, and to pop a plastic shopping bag over the whole to prevent any splashes on nearby walls. After four or five days the ferment will have quietened and you can have a final clean-up and insert a 'proper' airlock.

I often have several gallon jars of wine fermenting at the same time in my warm cupboard and I then economise on traps by using a length of plastic tubing leading from the bung of each jar into one common milk bottle half filled with sulphite solution.

Some winemakers content themselves with plugging the neck of the fermentation jar with cotton wool throughout, but I have reservations about this. It is an excellent idea for the first few days of fermentation, when the yeast needs plenty of oxygen to multiply, and when the use of cotton wool may simplify tidying up if you have an overvigorous, frothy fermentation, but it is not good practice thereafter. As the fermentation slows, and the amount of carbon dioxide given off decreases, the possibility of infection by airborne bacteria *increases*, and there is no visual indication as to how the fermentation is progressing. So it is always wise to employ some form of airlock, however primitive.

Yeasts

The essential thing to realise about winemaking is that the most important and central factor is the YEAST. The scientific name for yeast is *Saccharomyces*, or sugar fungus. Baker's yeast is *S. cerevisiae*, and true wine yeasts are *S. cerevisiae* var. *ellipsoideus*. The whole of winemaking practice really comes down to the matter of providing ideal conditions for the yeast, a living organism, to thrive and multiply. To do that the yeast must have sugar, it must have warmth, it must have oxygen, it must have a certain amount of nitrogenous matter, vitamins, and some acid. The ideal 'recipe' will provide all of these; if any one of them is lacking the ferment may 'stick', or temporarily stop.

Wine yeasts

One of the big strides which has been made in winemaking is that there are now available to the amateur many excellent varieties of special wine yeasts, in either culture or tablet form. Their value is unquestioned, for there are innumerable varieties of yeasts, all with different characteristics, and just as some are more suitable for baking or beer-brewing, so others are better for the production of quality wine. A good wine yeast has a high alcohol tolerance i.e. it will allow the wine to ferment further and be that much stronger before it succumbs. It will form a firmer sediment, making racking much simpler, and it will be less prone to impart 'off' flavours to the wine.

It is possible to obtain Port, Sherry, Beaujolais, Tokay, Chablis, Champagne, Sauternes, Bordeaux and Burgundy yeasts, to mention only a few.

These yeasts are laboratory-cultured from the yeasts on the grapes in the place of origin, and it is great fun to experiment with them, and see the different nuances of flavour than they confer.

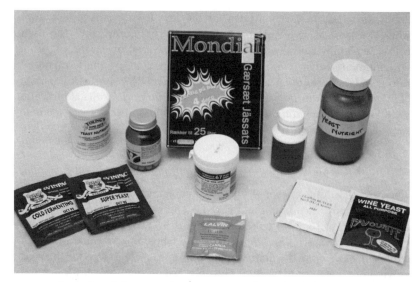

Just a few of the many wine yeasts now on the market. With them (except Mondial) use a good nutrient and vitamin B_1 tablets.

But do not imagine that you will obtain, say, a Port simply by using a Port yeast. The ingredients must be suitable as well. If they are, you are certainly more likely to obtain a port-like wine by using a true Port yeast; the flavour will be unimpaired, and you will have the other advantages already mentioned.

It is naturally advisable, when using these specialised yeasts, to employ them in 'musts' which will be sympathetic to them, i.e. a Port or Burgundy yeast in a red wine such as elderberry, sloe or damson, and a Champagne yeast in a sparkling wine. The beginner will do best, however, to experiment first with a good general-purpose wine yeast. You can also obtain a fairly good range of yeasts especially suitable for lager, beers and ales.

Many winemakers still adhere to baker's or brewer's yeasts, but it is a pity to do so without having tried some of the excellent true wine yeasts now on the market. They are certainly worthwhile for one's 'special' wines and are by no means as expensive as they at first appear, since they can be propagated and carried on from one wine to another. Wine yeast, granulated yeast, yeast cultures, yeast tablets, baker's yeasts, brewer's yeasts . . . all will make wine of varying quality, and which yeast you use is a matter of personal preference.

Wine yeasts are sold in various forms, granulated, as tablets, and as compounds complete with nutrients (e.g. Formula 67). Many of them nowadays are so good that they can be added direct to the must, and the fermentation will get going right away, just as it does with baker's yeast.

Baker's yeast, brewer's yeast or granulated domestic yeast can certainly be added direct to the must, when the liquid is lukewarm (about 21°C). They will give you a vigorous and frothy ferment, which is very encouraging if you are a beginner in that you will know the ferment really *has* got going, but it does not make for high-quality wine. Much of the wine's possible bouquet will be carried off with the rush of gas generated. If you wish to use such yeast, use it at the rate of 1 level teaspoonful per gallon.

But I firmly recommend you to start straight away with wine yeasts. The fermentation will be much less 'showy', and sometimes only just discernible as tiny bubbles round the periphery of the liquid in the jar, or by the movement in the airlock, but better wine will result.

Beginners often worry about exactly how much yeast to add but as long as you have enough to get the fermentation going reasonably quickly the quantity is not critical, since the first thing the yeast does is to multiply rapidly. Thus, when making, say, five gallons, you do not necessarily need five times as much yeast as for one. Either make up a starter bottle (see below), or, if you are adding the yeast direct to the must, double or treble the quantity. Individual suppliers provide detailed instructions with their yeasts, so there is no need to worry; you will find it quite simple. Initially go for a good general-purpose wine yeast such as C.W.E.'s Formula 67, Condessa's, Boots, Vinkwik, Unican, Vinpac, Gervin, Ritchie, Young's, or Brewicon and you should have no trouble.

Making up a starter bottle

So much work has been put into yeasts' development that in most cases they can be bought comparatively cheaply in a granular form which permits of their being added direct to the must. Most modern wine yeasts are supplied in sealed aluminium foil sachets, which ensure that the fine grains of yeast will not deteriorate or become contaminated in any way while in store. In most instances, direct addition to the must is acceptable, but a faster start to the fermentation can be achieved by sprinkling the yeast into two thirds of a cup of lukewarm water, covering it with a piece of clingfilm, and leaving it for 15 – 20 minutes. Then give it a stir and add it to the must. This revives the dormant yeast and the fermentation quickly gets under way.

Sometimes, however, you may wish to use a specialised wine yeast, of which you only receive a small quantity, to start say five or ten gallons. The yeast would achieve this in time, but to save the must from being available for invasion by spoilage organisms, it is better practice to activate the yeast, and increase the quantity of yeast at the same time. This is done by starting the yeast two days beforehand, in a specially prepared bottle of diluted fruit juice of some sort, sterilised by boiling and cooled, and a pinch of nutrient. When the contents of the bottle are fermenting vigorously they can be added to the must. Some of the starter bottle can be kept back, topped up with more fruit juice, plugged with cotton wool, and kept warm until fermenting again. It can then be stored in the fridge until required for your next brew, when it should be brought into the warm for a few hours before adding it to the must.

For the starter juice, you can use either the juice from which the wine is to be made (if some can be obtained beforehand) or another juice. As only half a pint at most will be required, after dilution with water, there will not be sufficient juice to affect the flavour of your wine. Dissolve an ounce of sugar and a pinch of nutrient in this, and sterilise it at the same time by bringing it to the boil. When cool, pour it into your starter bottle, and add the yeast. Seal with cotton wool or a piece of clingfilm.

Keep the bottle warm for a couple of days, when the presence of clouding in the juice, and tiny bubbles around the rim of the liquid will show fermentation is well under way. The starter can then be given a good shake to disperse the yeast through the liquid, and poured into the wine must. There may then be a lag period of up to two or three days, for the bulk fermentation to get under way, and for the carbon dioxide pressure to build up sufficiently to make the airlock start 'bubbling'.

Another good starter is a tablespoonful of pure malt extract, a tablespoonful of granulated sugar, the juice of a lemon, and half a pint of water, boiled together.

'No yeast' recipes

Incidentally, beware of all recipes which omit mention of yeast; there is no such thing as a 'no yeast' recipe for the simple reason that without yeast there can be no fermentation of the sort we want. Yeasts are everywhere about us – in the air, in the soil, the bloom on fruit, in milk, in our mouths – and will find their way into a fermentable liquor. If you use a 'no yeast' recipe, you are really simply relying upon any natural yeast which may be on the fruit you used or, if you killed that with boiling water or sulphite, upon any airborne yeast which may find its way into your brew . . . you *may* get a fermentation but the result may be not at all what you hope.

How yeast nutrient helps

To obtain the best possible fermentation the yeast, like most living organisms, must have both food and oxygen. Like human beings, it needs both vitamins and fresh air! The ideal medium for fermentation is pure grape juice, which contains all the nutrients, or foods, that the yeast requires, but some of the musts we ferment for country wines (notably mead and all the flower wines) are deficient in them, and it is therefore wise to add a nutrient to give the yeast a 'boost', the nitrogenous matter mentioned previously.

You can obtain several good proprietary yeast nutrients from trade sources, but if you are likely to be making wine regularly and in reasonable quantities, it will pay you to make up your own. Buy a 250 g jar of ammonium sulphate BP $(NH_4)_2SO_4$ and one of ammonium phosphate $(NH_4)_3PO_4$ and use half a level teaspoon of each in each gallon of wine. This will provide all the nitrogen and phosphate that the yeast needs, and the chemicals will always be ready to hand in your cupboard.

The other invaluable nutrient which has a wonderful effect upon the vigour of a fermentation is Vitamin B_1, or thiamine, as you can quite easily prove for yourself by adding it to some trial gallons. Buy it as tiny tablets (3 milligram size) from your chemist (they are sold under various brand names, such as Benerva) and use them regularly at the following rates per gallon:

Fruit wines	1 tablet
Grain, root, leaf and vegetable wines	2 tablets
Flower wines	3 tablets

This addition of nutrient to the must does certainly enable the yeast to carry the fermentation just that little further, and is a great help in the production of strong, *dry* wines, and in the avoidance of oversweet wines.

Other good general purpose nutrients to have by you are potassium phosphate and magnesium sulphate. Often, too, plain malt extract (not the cod liver oil variety!) can be used advantageously at the rate of one dessertspoon per gallon to get a fermentation away to a vigorous start, but it is wisest to restrict this practice to red or dark, full-flavoured wines, since it will impair the flavour and colour of light, delicate ones.

Sugars

For all normal winemaking (i.e. unless you want to affect the taste, bouquet or colour in a special way) use ordinary white household sugar (sucrose). It does not matter whether it is derived from cane or beet, chemically they are identical. There is no advantage (and some disadvantages) in using more expensive types.

Many old recipes specify candy sugar, but this is a hangover from the days when most sugar was unrefined and this was the best quality obtainable. Nowadays there is little to choose, for all practical purposes, between modern refined beet or cane sugars; they are all of excellent quality. Brown or Demerara sugar will impart a golden colour to a wine. It is therefore sometimes used to colour a uninteresting-looking wine, but it should not be used with wines where you wish to retain a delicate, natural colour from, say, a flower. It will also impart a slight flavour.

'Invert' sugar is not now available to winemakers. When yeast sets to work upon household sugar, or sucrose, it first splits it into its two main components, glucose and fructose, or 'inverts' it. In 'invert' sugar this has already been accomplished chemically, so that the yeast can start immediately to use the glucose (the principal sugar found in grapes). Thus by using 'invert' one may well obtain improved fermentation, improved to the extent that the yeast does not itself have to effect the inversion. 'Invert' will ferment more quickly than household sugar, and is widely used in the brewing industry. You can easily make it yourself by boiling 4 kilos (8 lb) of sugar in 1 litre (2 pints) of water with ½ teaspoon citric acid or tartaric acid. Bring it to the boil, stirring for half an hour. Add water to make up to 4.5 litres (1 gallon). There are 400 g of sugar in each 500 ml (1 lb in each pint).

Pure glucose, or grape sugar, can also now be purchased, and 18 oz of it will replace 16 oz of sucrose; it is naturally slightly more expensive than ordinary domestic sugar. Honey, of course, can also be employed to produce mead-flavoured wines. With liquid honey or thick, crystalline honey use pound for pound.

How much sugar to use? Many old recipes advocate far too much, with the result that winemakers are disappointed when the yeast fails to use most of it up, and they are left with a syrupy, almost undrinkable concoction. Often, too, winemakers fall into error because they do not realise the difference between sugar *to* the gallon and sugar *in* the gallon. 'To' the gallon means that one takes a gallon of liquid and adds the sugar to it, the resultant quantity being more than 1 gallon. 'In the gallon' means that one takes a 1-gallon jar or measure, puts the sugar in it, and then fills up to the 1-gallon mark. The latter system produces an exact gallon and uses less sugar, of course.

As a good rule of thumb, remember the figure 3; 3 lb to the gallon of liquor for a medium wine. Half a pound less will usually produce a dry wine, half a pound more a sweet. Below 2 lb of sugar to the gallon the wine may not be strong enough to keep, above 3½ it may well (although not always) be sickly sweet.

To the gallon
So remember – 2½ lb, dry; 3 lb, medium; 3½ lb sweet
Or, per litre – 250 g, dry; 300 g, medium; 350 g, sweet

In the gallon
So remember – 2 lb, dry; 2½ lb, medium; 3 lb, sweet
Or, per litre – 200 g, dry; 280 g, medium; 290 g, sweet

My own rule of thumb, making wines for my own use or experimenting with a new main ingredient, is to use 1 kilo of sugar (convenient in that it is one bag) *in* the gallon. This invariably produces a dry wine (which is generally to my taste) but which, if required, can be sweetened carefully with a non-fermentable sweetener such as Vinsweet, Sorbitol, Canderel or Sweetex.

One point, however, is all-important and must not be overlooked, and that is that there is natural sugar present in many of the ingredients that we use. Often, at the dilutions that we practise, the amount in a gallon will be negligible, but with certain fruits it can be enough for us to have to take it into account in our calculations. It is therefore necessary, when preparing such wines to one's own recipe, to take the SG of the must (see 'The Hydrometer') and calculate how much sugar in or to the gallon that represents. That amount can then be deducted from the weight of sucrose used.

When trying to make really strong, sweet dessert wines it is a good idea, since it eases the task of the yeast and makes for better fermentation, to add the sugar in stages, half the total quantity at the outset, and the remainder by stages in 4 oz lots each time the ferment slows or the SG drops to 1005 (see 'The Hydrometer', p. 76).

Draw off a pint or so of the wine, dissolve the sugar in it by stirring thoroughly (use no heat or you will kill the yeast) and restore the sweetened quantity to the main bulk of the wine. Any undissolved sugar in the wine may cause the ferment to 'stick'. Caster sugar dissolves most easily.

If you wish to avoid this risk add the later amounts of sugar in 2 oz   35 or 4 oz doses as a strong syrup, made by dissolving 1 lb in half a pint (450 g in 280 ml) of boiling water, which is then cooled. This syrup has a gravity (q.v.) of 300, and 1 pint equals 1 lb sugar.

Some useful sugar facts:

1 pint (568 ml) syrup = 1 lb (454 g) sugar
1 pint = 40 tablespoons
1 tablespoon = ½ fl oz (15 ml)
2½ tablespoons (37.5 ml) syrup = 1 oz (28 g) sugar
So 2 oz sugar = 5 tablespoons syrup
So 4 oz sugar = 10 tablespoons syrup

These doses can be used to 'feed' the tail-end of a fermentation when a strong, sweet wine is desired. The last dose added will probably remain in the wine as a sweetener.

When starting a wine off it is always better to use little sugar rather than too much, because dry wine can always be sweetened, but there is little you can really do about a wine which is oversweet, other than blend it with a dry one of the same type. And there is nothing more off-putting to your true wine lover than a wine which is horribly oversweet (though correctly-sweet wines are agreeable in the right context, of course).

If you are making a heavy-bodied, sweet dessert wine more of the basic ingredients will need to be added when putting it together to balance its extra sweetness, but it is still as well to keep the initial sugar level to that for a dry wine and to add the balance of the sugar later, preferably as syrup. If you decide to sugar a finished wine and are afraid this may start it fermenting again, add one Campden tablet and 1 g of potassium sorbate per gallon to prevent this occurring. Or you can use for the purpose one of the sweeteners such as Sorbitol, which are non-fermentable by wine yeasts and therefore cause no fermentation.

Potassium sorbate is an excellent stabiliser. A simple way of measuring 1 gram is to dissolve 1 oz in 15 fl oz water, which has been boiled and cooled – ½ fl oz will then contain 1 gram. To avoid bacterial infection, you must always add a Campden tablet at the same time.

Getting the flavour

There are several ways of extracting the required flavour from our fruit or vegetables – pressing, using juice extractors, or boiling, soaking in hot or cold water, and fermenting on the 'pulp' – and there are advantages to each; which you use depends on the wine being made and the equipment

Two excellent small winepresses, each adequate for most home winemakers.

available (which usually means how much you are prepared to spend!).

Sometimes you first extract the juice from all the ingredients and start the fermentation right away. The straight juice may be fermented, but for reasons of economy (to avoid using too large a quantity of fruit) and so as not to have too strong a flavour, it is more usual for the juice to be diluted with water.

Alternatively, the fruit is pulped, the 'must' prepared, and the yeast introduced, so that the fermentation begins immediately, and the liquor is not strained from the solids until, say, 10 days later. This is more convenient for those who do not wish to buy the more expensive equipment, and is also used when it is desired to extract colour from the skins of fruit or from the fruit itself (as when making red grape wine). Whichever system is used, the quantities advocated in the recipes remain the same.

In the latter case it is a great help to extraction to add 1 teaspoon of a pectin-destroying enzyme such as Rohament P, Pektolase or Pectinol, to hasten the breakdown of the fruit (and, incidentally, ensure a clear wine). It should be added 24 hours before the yeast, and only when the 'must' or juice is cool or cold. (Boiling water will destroy the enzyme.) For maximum *flavour* release Rohament P, which has a near-miraculous action, should be used at room temperature for up to 24 hours and for maximum *colour* release for 1 – 2 hours at 40°C. It is not, however, suitable for producing a clear juice, so for winemaking Pectinol should be used simultaneously or subsequently. Both preparations are used at the rate of 2.5 g to 6 lb fruit.

It is particularly important to use such a pectin destroying enzyme with fruits or vegetables which are high in pectin, e.g. parsnips, carrots, damsons, plums, gooseberries, blackcurrants, loganberries, blackberries, apples and pears, and citrus fruits. With a medium pectin content are peaches, apricots, beetroot, raspberry, rhubarb, and strawberry (which is why pectin is added in jam making), followed by low pectin ingredients such as grapes, cherries, pineapple, bilberries and elderberries.

Pressing

A large press is only necessary if you are going to tackle large quantities. A small one like that on the right will satisfy most winemakers.

Pressing is ideal for grapes (which must first be broken), fruit and berries. Even if you cannot afford the luxury of a proper press – and they are not expensive now – it is well worth contriving one of your own or borrowing one from your winemaking club. I have found that the ideal combination for the serious winemaker is some sort of fruit crusher with which to mash the fruit, and a medium-sized press with which to press it: these will deal effectively with almost anything, even, say, a hundredweight of apples. Do not rush the pressing, and pass the juice straight through a sieve and funnel into a 1-gallon jar. For pre-pulping fruit a Pulpmaster electric drill attachment or a kitchen food processor is useful; or you can chop the fruit with a heavy Chinese chopper or even the head of a kindling axe.

If you are not using too large quantities of fruit, it can be deep frozen for a minimum of a day (longer if you wish) in any part of your freezer, then thawed and pressed. This softens the fruit, and gives a better than average yield of juice. The juice can then be re-frozen if you wish (ice cream cartons are suitable) and stored until you wish to make wine from them. This does save space in the freezer.

Extractors

The modern way. Juice extractors can now be obtained quite cheaply and range from the simple, hand-operated one which is a development of the old-fashioned mincer to sophisticated, powerful electric models such as the Kenwood, Beekay and Moulinex food processors. With most of the makes available you use 1 or 2 lb of fruit at a time. It is effortless, but the filter has to be cleaned out after every 4 or 5 lb and this becomes tedious when doing larger quantities. If you can find one which ejects pulp and juice separately, it is far more satisfactory, since it does not clog so quickly.

Cheaper than these, or than a press, is a steam extractor, and this, like the others, will separate the juice from the pulp most efficiently. Again, this is a really excellent system for dealing with smaller quantities of a few pounds of fruit or vegetables, and a real delight in that it is so clean and delivers sterile juice, but I find it rather slow and tedious if handling larger quantities. This is because each time you reload with fruit there is an appreciable delay before juice starts to run, even if boiling water is used.

Boiling

Boiling (necessary with some root and fruit wines) is a method that has to be used with care, for if the ingredients (particularly parsnips and plums) are overboiled it may later prove difficult to get the wine to clear. The liquor is then strained off the solids, cooled and fermented.

Cold water soaking

The fruit is pulped or the 'must' prepared, the yeast is introduced, and the liquor is not strained from the solids until, say, 5 to 7 days later. This can be used with hard fruit as a preliminary to pressing. All you really need is a large brew-bin or a bucket. Again, the use of an enzyme helps greatly.

Hot water soaking

Boiling or near-boiling water may be poured over the ingredients, which are then left to soak for three or four days, the yeast having been introduced when the 'must' has cooled to 21°C. The liquor is then strained off.

Where boiling water is used the 'must' will have been purified, for any wild yeast which may have been present will have been killed, but if pressing or the cold water method are employed it is as well to add one Campden tablet per gallon, and to wait 24 hours before adding your chosen yeast. The sulphur dioxide of the tablet will dispose of unwanted wild yeasts but 24 hours later its action will have abated sufficiently to allow your selected yeast to start working satisfactorily.

When, by one of these means, the flavour has been extracted, the sugar is added and the yeast and yeast nutrient introduced in order to cause fermentation, and the fermentation is then conducted as described later.

Acidity

Acidity is usually quoted as parts per thousand (ppt) in terms of sulphuric acid, but sulphuric acid is not used in winemaking (heaven forbid!) but merely provides a handy comparative scale with those acids which we do use. See conversion factors under 'Titration' (p. 43). Estimate how much you need according to the fruit you are using, and as a rule of thumb remember that fruits of medium acidity will require two *level* teaspoons of citric acid per gallon. Low and very low acid ingredients will require more, and high or very high, less or none at all. As a guide to the acid to add to popular ingredients:

Very low   Beet, dates, figs, flowers, all grain, leaves, parsnips, rosehips –
3 teaspoons.

Chopping apples with a kindling axe blade prior to juicing them in the steam extractor.   41

Low   Bananas, dried fruits, elderberries, pears, pineapple – *2½ teaspoons.*

Medium   Apples, apricots, cherries, concentrates, damsons, grapes, greengages, nectarines, oranges, peaches, plums – *2 teaspoons.*

High   Bilberries, blackberries, gooseberries, loganberries, quinces, raspberries, rowanberries, strawberries, worcesterberries – *1 teaspoon.*

Very high   Blackcurrants, grapefruit, lemons, limes, cherries (Morello), red currants, rhubarb, white currants – *None.*

But remember that the acidity of a *finished* wine can always be adjusted, though admittedly it is easier to add more acid than to remove any over-acidity chemically or by dilution or blending. You may prefer to use the rule of thumb of adding sufficient acid to ensure a healthy fermentation, say two *level* teaspoons per gallon, and make any necessary adjustment when you assess the finished wine.

Acids used in winemaking

Citric acid

Occurs in bananas, red and white currants, elderberries, grapefruit, lemons, limes, loganberries, oranges, pears, pineapples, raspberries, strawberries and tangerines, and is the most popular single acid, since it imparts brilliance, is stable, and has a pleasant, fruity flavour. If you want to keep things simple and use just one acid, plump for citric.

Malic acid

Is found in apples, apricots, blackberries, bullaces, cherries, damsons, greengages, gooseberries, nectarines, peaches, plums, rhubarb, rowan-berries, sloes (and in some wine kits) – and seems to have the virtue of helping to speed fermentation. Malic acid predominates in rhubarb; poisonous oxalic acid is mainly confined to the leaves.

Tartaric acid

Is that found in the grape (or raisins, sultanas and currants) and is said to improve the vinous character of the wine, but is often unstable, any excess being thrown out of solution in the wine as tartrate crystals. Incidentally, although tartaric is the principal acid in grapes, there is usually a high proportion of malic also.

The acids are not confined to these fruits and are often found alongside one another in varying quantities, a little citric where malic predominates, and vice versa, for instance.

Succinic acid

Small quantities of succinic acid added late in fermentation are often found to improve a wine's bouquet and maturation processes.

Acid mix

Many winemakers nowadays use a 'mix' of acids, and I would recommend the following:

Citric	1 part
Malic	2 parts
Tartaric	3 parts

Easy to remember: C, M, T (alphabetical order) and 1 – 2 – 3!

Use 1 – 3 level teaspoons per gallon according to the acidity or lack of acidity of the main ingredient.

Titration

How do we measure acidity? There is only one really satisfactory way, and that is by titration, which gives us the answer as parts per thousand in terms of sulphuric acid, but in my experience of winemakers all over the country, it is not very popular. Understandably, few own, or can be bothered to buy, a burette and stand and do the test in the laboratory manner. But kits for this purpose can be purchased for as little as £2.50 and it is a pity that more winemakers do not avail themselves of these simple kits to get the all-important acidity level right.

Acid titration is carried out by placing 10 ml of must in a test tube. Use a small syringe to measure quantities. Add 100 ml of distilled water, and 2 or 3 drops of Phenolpthalein. Shake well to mix.

Take another syringe and fill it with N10 (decinormal) solution of sodium hydroxide. Be careful when handling this solution as it is very caustic. Drip it drop by drop into the test-tube, shaking gently. The solution will turn pink, but by shaking the tube it will return to normal. Repeat, adding the sodium hydroxide one drop at a time, until a stable pink is produced which does not fade when shaken.

43

Read off from the syringe the number of millilitres of sodium hydroxide you have used. This equals the parts per thousand of acid in the wine, *measured in terms of sulphuric acid*. This acid is only used as a standard, and must never be added to the wine. To convert this figure to malic or citric acid, multiply by 1.4, for tartaric, probably the most useful, by 1.5.

If you need then to *raise* the acidity, remember that ⅛ oz (3.6 g) of citric acid (or the mix) will raise the acidity of 1 gallon (4.5 litres) by 0.5 ppt.

If you need to *reduce* the acidity ¼ oz (6 g) of potassium carbonate will reduce the acidity of 1 gallon (4.5 litres) by 1 ppt.

With strong, well-flavoured and robust wines a reduction can often be achieved satisfactorily by simple dilution.

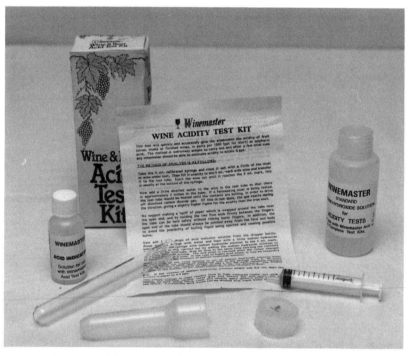

A simple and inexpensive testing kit like this will enable you to determine the acidity of your musts and wines with accuracy, perhaps the most important single factor in quality.

Measuring pH

There *is* another way to assess the acidity of a wine or must, and that is by measuring its pH (hydrogen ion concentration). This indicates the strength or intensity of the acid present by means of narrow range papers (1 – 14) like the Litmus papers you used at school. Just dip them in the must or wine, and when the paper changes colour compare it with the chart provided and read off the pH. Remember that the pH of an acid solution is always *less* than 7: the lower the pH the higher the acidity. The optimum figure is 3.2 but anywhere in the range 3.0 – 3.4 is acceptable.

The only trouble is that although this method is simple it is not too accurate because of the buffer effect of musts and wines, which means that there is no direct correlation between pH and acidity. But pH, like taste, is quite a good guide, and many winemakers like this method for its simplicity.

Tannin

A small quantity of tannin will vastly improve the taste of most wines, giving them a zest or bite which is otherwise lacking, particularly in flower, root and grain wines. It is the tannin in a wine which gives an impression of dryness in the mouth after drinking; if the right amount of tannin is present, the wine will be supple and zestful; if too little, flat, insipid and characterless; if too much, harsh, astringent and bitter. Tannin is also an essential constituent if a wine is to have good keeping qualities.

Tannins come from the skins and stems of fruit – particularly red fruit, and wines made from all red fruit and from elderberries, bilberries, sloes, damsons, plums, apples, pears, grapes, and oak leaves are liable to be rich in tannin, and usually need none added. In flower and grain wines add one teaspoon (5 ml) of grape tannin, a few oak leaves or pear peelings, or one tablespoonful of strong tea per gallon; half a teaspoon or less is required in other wines. It is not really practicable for the amateur to test for tannin content.

Sometimes, particularly with elderberry wines, there is an excess of tannin and sometimes with other wines the same effect is created by using too much fruit, by soaking for too long a period, or pressing too hard. If a finished wine is a little too harsh, it can often be vastly improved by the addition of a little sugar or glycerine, but if it is far too harsh it should be fined with gelatine or blended with another softer wine.

Water

Ordinary tap water in Britain is quite safe and satisfactory for winemaking, though really hard, i.e. chalky, water may be better for being boiled.

Conducting your fermentation

Now let us get on with the making of an orthodox country wine. If you are fermenting a juice, or a liquor with no solid ingredients left in it, it can well go straight into a fermenting jar which, however, should not be filled beyond the shoulder, and a fermentation trap fitted. (If you fill your jar the ferment, in its first vigour, will foam out through the trap.)

The yeast and yeast nutrient are added at the same time and the jar is placed in a warm place, about 21°C (70°F). A warm kitchen is ideal, but do *not* stand the jar on a stove or anywhere it is likely to be *over* heated,

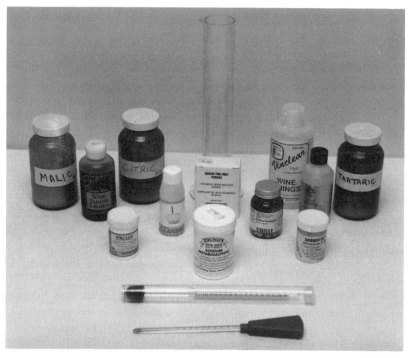

Some suggestions for your wine cupboard – thermometer, hydrometer and test jar, sodium metabisulphite, malic acid, citric acid, tartaric acid, finings, tannin, stabilisers and Vitamin B tablets.

or the yeast may be killed, and fit either a cotton wool plug or an airlock. After four or five days or so the ferment will quieten, and the jar should be 'topped up' to the bottom of the neck either with some of the liquor or with syrup of the same strength as the original liquor. The airlock, of course, is again fitted.

It is good practice to use all the ingredients for one gallon of must, but make up initially only six to seven pints, which can then be topped up

Heating pads like these, manufactured by Thorne Electrim, are an excellent means of holding fermentations at a steady temperature. They are made in 1, 2, 4 and 6 gallon sizes.

My own simple fermentation cupboard is warmed by a short length of pipe of the central heating system from the adjacent boiler (r.)

later with water to the full gallon. But if you have made up a full gallon or more of must, and need to leave a headspace in the gallon jar for the first week or so, put the balance of the juice into a bottle or smaller jar, with a pinch of yeast, and fit an airlock or cotton wool plug. It can then be used to top up the gallon jar as soon as the ferment quietens (about a week), or after the first racking.

The jar is then best kept at a temperature of 16–18°C (60–65°F) until fermentation is finished. Check it regularly, particularly if you are adding sugar by stages, and watch both specific gravity and the airlock action.

It helps to agitate the jar occasionally by giving it a shake. Be careful to avoid big temperature changes or draughts, but do not fuss too much: wine will ferment quite happily in the average living room, kitchen or centrally heated house. The temperature is not critical but fluctuations are.

If your wine has to ferment in an unheated room or shed you can still maintain a satisfactory temperature by using one of the electric heating pads or belts sold by winemaking shops, or by building yourself an insulated warm box or fermentation cupboard. The absolute minimum of heat is required.

When the ferment appears to have finished, move it back into a warm room for a few days to see if it restarts.

If you are dealing with a 'must' with a large quantity of solid ingredients you will probably find that, at least for the first 7 days or so after the yeast has been added, because of the great bulk, it will probably be necessary to use a container such as a polythene bucket or fermenting bin. This must be closely covered with several thicknesses of cloth or a sheet of polythene secured with elastic to keep infection at bay. If it is a cold water soaking, sulphite must be added 24 hours before the yeast. Again ... a temperature of 21°C (70°F). Do not forget to stir the 'must' from the bottom twice daily.

At the end of the soaking period strain off the liquor through a nylon sieve, a straining bag, or two or three thicknesses of muslin – do it thoroughly and do not hurry it – into your fermenting jar and fit your airlock, carrying on thereafter as above.

Stuck ferments

If you have used the right amount of sugar and fermentation has apparently ceased too soon (the wine will be oversweet and its specific gravity too high) the fermentation is said to have 'stuck'.

First racking for a wine which has been fermented in a 1-gallon jar.

Possible causes:

Poor quality yeast
Too high or too low a temperature
The yeast has reached its limit of alcohol tolerance (i.e. the wine is finished)
The sugar has all been utilised (add more)
Too much sugar (dilute slightly)
Insufficient nutrient or acid (add more)
Insufficient oxygen (aerate by stirring and pouring)
Too much carbon dioxide (uncork and stir)

A good general-purpose 'booster' for stuck wine is:
½ teaspoon diammonium phosphate
Tip of teaspoon of magnesium sulphate (Epsom salts)
1 × 3 mg tablet Vitamin B (Benerva)

The simplest solution is to add some 'Restart', a high-powered yeast from Condessa, but if this and all other remedies fail, make up a half pint starter with the juice of three oranges, water, 1 level dessertspoon sugar, yeast, and a pinch of nutrient. Get it going well, then add an equal quantity of the 'stuck' wine. When all this is fermenting, again add an equal quantity of the wine and continue 'doubling up' in this way until all is fermenting once more.

Note that with a dry wine the final SG (see 'The Hydrometer' p. 76) will be well *below* 1000, say 995 or 996, because the alcohol which has been produced is lighter than water and will therefore 'dilute' the water, which has an SG of 1000.

Racking

One of the most important factors in producing clear, stable wine is racking, i.e. siphoning the wine off the lees of yeast and deposited solids; more wines have been ruined by neglect of racking than from any other cause. During the first fermentation a wine will be milky and soupy – and often downright repulsive! – in appearance, and no one would imagine that one day it will be brilliantly clear, and perhaps even sparkling. But do not dismay. Properly made, and properly managed subsequently, almost all wines will clear of their own accord. Some wines, parsnip and plum among them, are notorious for their slowness to clear, and it should be noted that it is usually where the ingredients have been boiled that this occurs, for boiling releases pectin to cause hazes in the wine. These hazes, however, should not be confused with the thick cloudiness of the early stages of fermentation.

A wine is likely to remain really cloudy for three or four months after the fermentation is started because of the yeast in suspension; then, slowly, it will commence to clear, from the top down, as the yeast and solids in it sink to the bottom, forming a thick layer at the bottom of the fermenting jar. When the wine has cleared in this way – rack.

Place a clean jar below the level of the one containing the wine, and remove the bung and airlock. Take a yard or so of PVC tubing (about $\frac{5}{16}$" diameter) and in one end of it fit a foot of glass, stainless steel, or rigid plastic tubing. Insert the tubing carefully into the wine (carefully so as not to disturb the sediment) to about half the depth of the jar, and hold it in place by clipping a wooden clothes peg around it, or by using a rubber band.

Take the lower end of the tube down to below the level of the bottom of the fermentation jar, put it into your mouth, and suck steadily (most pleasant, this!). You can buy more sophisticated siphons which will start the flow for you, but it seems a pity to deprive yourself of a taste! When the wine is flowing freely direct it into a new jar. As the level in the fermentation jar drops push the tube down further and further until you have racked off all the wine and only the yeast sediment is left. Be careful not to siphon that into the new jar.

Before fitting the airlock to your new jar of semi-clear wine, make sure that the jar is filled to the bottom of the neck, so that the minimum of air is allowed access to the wine.

Do this by 'topping up' if necessary (and it usually is) with syrup, made to the same strength as your original 'must'. Thus, if your original 'must' had 3 lb of sugar to the gallon (48 oz) use 3 oz of sugar in half a pint of water. Or use surplus must as previously described.

Then insert your airlock and allow the fermentation to proceed again. At first it will probably be much slower than previously, but do not worry about this; it is because the quantity of yeast present has been greatly reduced. As the yeast gradually multiplies again so the ferment will get going once more, and a slow, steady ferment, rather than a fast one, is what you want.

The wine will also continue to clear, and the yeast will throw a second deposit. When the wine is *completely* clear, and the sediment is firm, comes the time for your second racking. This time 'top up' with other wine or brandy, or water if you intend to enter shows, and not with syrup or you may get an interminable fermentation. (The yeast left behind on this occasion will be an excellent medium for starting off other brews.)

You may care to bottle on this occasion, but it is preferable to give the wine yet a third racking after another two months before doing so. Normally about three months elapse between first and second rackings but it is impossible to give a firm schedule since the time to rack depends upon the progress of the individual wine.

Racking rarely harms a wine, and generally improves it; racking helps to stabilise the wine, thus reducing the risk of after-bottling fermentation and consequent burst bottles. Racking also prevents the wine acquiring 'off' flavours from the dead yeast upon which it would otherwise be standing.

Always make sure that your fermentation is completely finished before bottling, or you may have burst bottles, which is both messy and dangerous. Most beginners fall into the error of trying to bottle too soon, and pay dearly for their mistake.

It always pays, for the same reason, to add sulphite at the rate of 50 ppm (1 crushed Campden tablet per gallon) or potassium sorbate at the rate of 1 g per gallon before bottling, i.e. at second or third racking. If you use potassium sorbate as a stabiliser, for which purpose it is excellent, note that one Campden tablet per gallon must also be used in conjunction with it, or the wine may acquire a 'geranium' smell.

Clearing

Normally a well-made wine will clear of its own accord, given time (which can be as much as a year in some cases) but when it does not, it may be necessary to resort to fining or filtering. The best advice that I can give, however, is *always* give your wine a chance to clear naturally. Avoid fining, which may upset the chemical balance of the wine, and filter only as a last resort, for filtering does take something out of a wine besides the murkiness.

Usually all that is necessary is to move the wine, at the end of fermentation, into a much lower temperature (say from a warm kitchen to a cold larder or outhouse, but *not* into a refrigerator). In some cases, if you have some clear wine of the same sort from the previous year, pouring some of this in on top of the new wine will rapidly clear it.

If your wine remains obstinately cloudy it is probably caused by:

(a) Pectin
(b) Starch or
(c) Protein

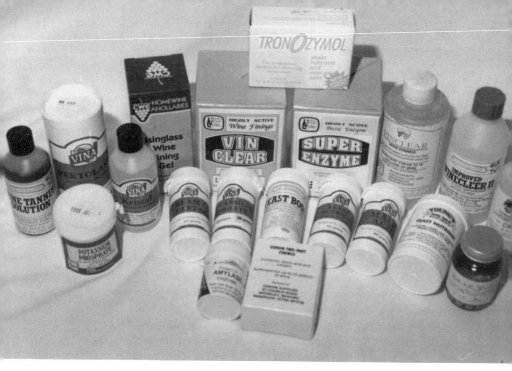

A selection of preparations that will ensure healthy fermentations and brilliantly clear wines.

Pectin

A pectin haze is better prevented than attempting to remove it by fining, which may make it worse, so always use a pectin enzyme with a pectin-containing fruit. Tiny jelly blobs which look rather like frogspawn surround haze particles, keeping them in suspension and defying the use of any fining. To check whether a haze is due to pectin add 100 ml (3 or 4 fl oz) of methylated spirit to 30 ml (1 fl oz) of wine. If jelly-like clots or strings are formed the haze is due to pectin and the wine should be treated with Pectinol. For each 4.5 litres (1 gallon) add 5 g (⅛ oz) to 280 ml (½ pint) wine, which is kept warm, 21–27°C, for 4 hours, stirring occasionally; strain through paper towel or muslin and add to the bulk of the wine. Leave the wine at 16–21°C for several days.

Starch

The effect is similar to that of pectin, but starch hazes usually occur in wines made from grain, bananas or root vegetables, so when making wine from these materials use a starch reducing enzyme such as Amylozyme to turn the non-fermentable starch into fermentable sugar. To test for starch take a small quantity of wine and apply a drop of ordinary iodine. The slightest trace of starch will produce an unmistakable blue colour. Remedy: treat with Fungal Amylase 2209 (10 per cent) or Diastase used at the rate of 2.5 g (1 teaspoon) to 20 litres (5 gallons).

Protein

If you have used enzymes initially but still get a haze it is probably due to protein, and this is best dealt with by fining. Protein particles have a minute positive charge and certain finings have minute negative charges. Since 'opposites attract' the two combine, making the protein particles heavier, causing them to sink and clearing the wine. (Protein test: add 2 ml of 5 per cent tannic acid to 35 ml of wine (1 part to 20 of wine). A cloudy deposit in 24 hours indicates fining is advisable).

The commercial wine world uses several types of fining, organic (gelatine, isinglass, egg whites, egg albumen powder, pure ox blood, casein, etc.), mineral (Bentonite, Kaolin or Kieselguhr) and vegetable (alkaline alginates), but some of these are risky in the hands of the amateur, since they require a reasonably exact dosage calculated as the result of experiments, and it is difficult to work down to the smaller quantities we usually need.

Many proprietary wine finings work on the simple principle that tannins and proteins precipitate one another and therefore add in turn some of each. Most winemakers prefer to play safe and buy some reliable proprietary finings, with detailed instructions. Quite the best general-purpose finings that I have come across is Harris Easifine or Winecleer, sold by Vina, which I have found to have a startling effect in a wide range of both white and red wines not of sufficient clarity. It is liquid *Chitin*, manufactured from the shells of shrimps and crabs, and it removes both pectin and starch, so that wines usually clear within 48 hours of treatment. It certainly seems to tackle most hazes, and the beauty of it is its ease of use: merely add between ¼ and ½ fl oz per gallon (10–20 ml per 5 litres) and then leave the wine for a couple of days. This is an excellent standby to have in your winery cupboard.

Another excellent 'general-purpose' way of clearing hazes from, and lending real clarity to, your wines is fining by means of *Bentonite* ($Al_2O_3.4S_iO_2.H_2O$), an effective clarifying and stabilising agent. A montmorillonite clay which can absorb ten times its own weight of water, with which it forms a gelatinous paste, it causes a coagulation of the proteins, which increases proportionately as the acidity of the wine is greater and the tannin content smaller, and its action appears almost miraculous.

It can be purchased from almost all the well-established and reputable home wine supplies firms, and should be used at the rate of ¼ oz of Bentonite to 3 fl oz of water (50 g to ½ litre). Since it will keep indefinitely, but has to be made up at least 24 hours before use, it pays to make up a quantity at a time, and preferably to do so at the outset in two smaller containers, so that when one is used up it can be immediately replenished, and the suspension in the second container will have been standing for weeks, or even months, and will be ready for use.

Use 1-pint bottles with flat bottoms and screw craps; fruit juice bottles are ideal. Into each bottle pour 9 fl oz of water (boiled and then cooled) and then funnel in ¾ oz of Bentonite. Screw on the cap and shake vigorously, impacting the liquid against the flat bottom of the bottle to force the Bentonite into suspension. Then leave the bottles for at least 24 hours, and preferably more, before use, to allow the montmorillonite particles to swell and become effective coagulators.

To use the suspension, remember that in each bottle you have ¾ oz of Bentonite. The advocated dose for all ordinary hazes or straightforward fining is one-eighth of an ounce per gallon of wine, and for really bad hazes ¼ oz, so you will need to use one-sixth of the contents for 'normal' fining, and one-third of the contents for really thick hazes. (Metric dose: 5 – 10 g per 5 litres.)

The wine should, of course, have been racked off any deposit. Draw off a little to make room for the suspension, measure out the 'dose' of Bentonite, pour it into the wine through a funnel, and top up as required with wine. Re-cork and then rotate or swirl the jar gently to mix the Bentonite into the wine. Keep it in suspension for at least 20 minutes by rocking and swirling at 3-minute intervals. Rack after a fortnight, *not* before.

Bentonite is a very versatile material. It can be added to a must at the beginning of a fermentation at the rate of a rounded teaspoonful of dry powder per gallon. It will absorb moisture during the fermentation, and while in the must, remove some of the unwanted proteins. The wine will drop perfectly clear at the end of fermentation, and the sediment will soon become a compact layer on the bottom of the demijohn, ready for racking.

You can also buy Bentonite in two other prepared forms. It is obtainable as a ready-made gel, with the water fully absorbed, that can be used at any stage, but preferably at the end of fermentation, or as prepared

Dismantled Harris Vinbrite filter

granules, that will absorb wine and be active straight away.

Finally, if you are in a hurry, and have only Bentonite powder to hand, you will find that it can be blended with alcohol much more rapidly than with water. So try stirring it into a little of your finished wine, and then when it is nice and creamy, blend it into your bulk wine.

Yet a third easily-made fining which works like magic on many wines – I cannot explain it scientifically, but can only affirm that it does – can be made from bananas which have gone black. Boil 0.5 kilo (1 lb) of peeled black bananas in 0.6 litres (1 pint) of water and strain off the juice. Add 100 ml (3–4 fl oz) to each 4.5 litres (1 gallon) of hazy wine.

The use of enzyme preparations and occasionally, fining, will usually ensure clear wines, but sometimes you may wish to achieve a further final brilliance, i.e. 'polishing' them as well, to bring them up to that brilliance which makes them really attractive and will carry off the prizes when they appear on a show bench.

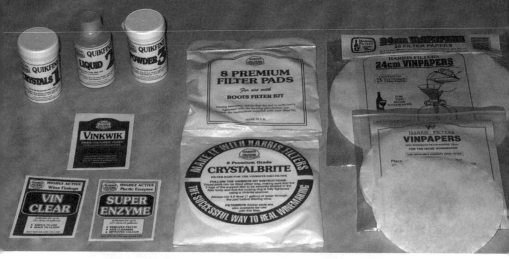

Harris offer a complete solution to clearing wines and beers comprising pectin treatment, finings and filter systems. beloe is shown the Buon Vino from Ritchies.

For this you can employ one of the superb proprietary filters now on the market, such as the Harris Major Mark II, or the Vinbrite, from Harris Filters, of Dudley, West Midlands, the Vinamat Filter system, or that from Boots plc, which is widely used. They all employ compressed discs or pads similar to those used in the commercial wine world. Modern

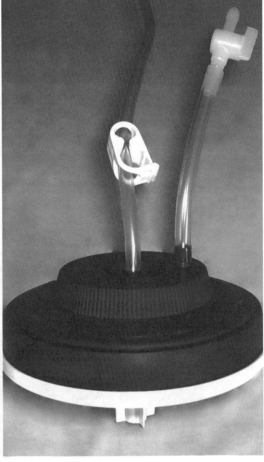

Two extremely efficient filters, both of which make use of powders, the Quikfine and the Harris.

filters, which will filter and polish wines to brilliance, use pads which contain no asbestos (once a popular filtering medium but now suspected of being a health threat). Harris also manufacture a Quikfine filter which achieves remarkable results by combining the action of gelatine, Bentonite and a filter bag, and which seems to cope with almost any wine, although it is slightly more complicated to use.

The Vinamat, in which air pressure is used to speed the flow.

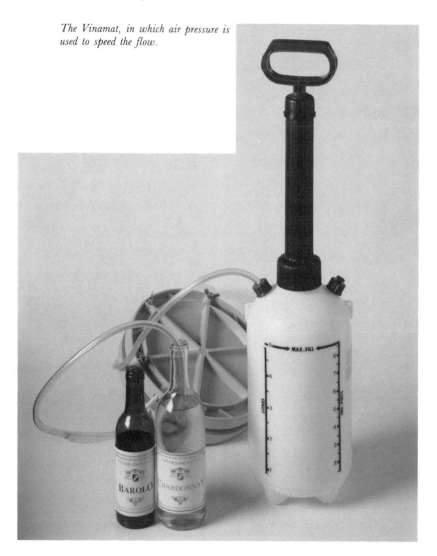

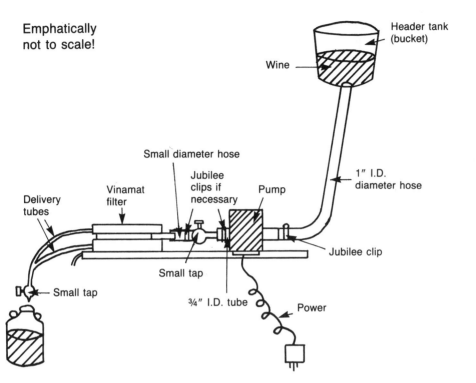

Emphatically not to scale!

Header tank (bucket)

Wine

Small diameter hose

Jubilee clips if necessary

Vinamat filter

Pump

Delivery tubes

1" I.D. diameter hose

Jubilee clip

Small tap

Small tap

¾" I.D. tube

Power

But if you can spare a bit more cash, invest in a Vinamat (from Ritchie Products Ltd, Burton on Trent) a really superb job which filters wine really rapidly under pressure through outside pads, and will speedily clear most brews; it's a delight to use – but costs over £50 (1995).

Since I use one of these filters quite regularly for 5-gallon batches of wine and have an inbuilt aversion to physical effort, I have eliminated the need for hand pumping every few minutes by converting an electric pump from a washing machine to do the job for me.

My method employs a plastic bucket as a header tank, placed on a stand which gives about a metre fall to the electric pump. The pump is one supplied for washing-machines, and you may pick one up cheaply second-hand. It must be fitted with a fused plug, and can be plugged straight into a mains socket fitted with a switch. Otherwise an on/off switch must be fitted in the cable before the pump. It is secured to a long base-plate, with raised edges to prevent any leakage overflows, and which also accommodates the Vinamat filter. This base was made to slope slightly, so that any leakage from the filter will drain to one corner, and through a drainage hole be collected in a jug for re-filtration.

The Vinamat hand pump was discarded. The one-metre feed tube needs to be of a suitable bore to accept the intake of the pump, and is secured with a screw thread and plastic nuts fitting through an appropriately-sized hole bored in the base of the bucket. To reduce the amount of lees left in the bucket to the minimum, slice the large nut (which is going inside the bucket) in half horizontally, and if necessary, use a suitable washer. (My pipe is of 1 inch internal diameter.) At the pump intake the tube was secured with a Jubilee clip. A smaller bore tube (¾" internal diam.), leads from the pump outlet to a wooden plug, secured with another Jubilee clip, which had been drilled to accept a short length of plastic tubing. This is interrupted by a second stopcock, and is a tight push fit onto the intake of the central ring of the Vinamat, between the two filter pads. The filter's normal delivery tubes were used, except that another small tap is fitted at the end, again to help keep control of the process.

The delivery pipe of the filter is fitted with a terminal tap fitted into a 1-gallon-jar-sized cork, which goes into the receiving jar. A slot cut into the side of the cork allows air to escape. The tap enables me to stop the filter momentarily to change jars without mess; for longer stops I switch the power off.

Because there is almost bound to be some splashing or leakage when doing a job of this kind, it is advisable to make some kind of cover for the pump. I made a light plywood case, drilled holes in it to allow air to circulate for cooling, and gave it two or three coats of varnish. Clip the wiring securely out of the way.

If you do not already have a Vinamat filter, your supplier should be able to obtain parts for you, thus saving the cost of the hand pump.

To operate the filter I usually pass a gallon of sulphited water through first, in case of any liquid remaining in the pump from the previous batch, and I always re-run the first quart or so (1 to 2 litres) of the wine. The system may take a little while to settle down and free itself of air bubbles, particularly when you are screwing down the securing bolts of the filter. If, when these are fully screwed home, you still have persistent trouble with air bubbles, you will need to break the system somewhere, usually between the pump and the filter. This can be minimised by ensuring that the wines you filter are free of dissolved carbon dioxide, a normal component of very young wines.

Normally, however, as long as you have adequate head pressure in the feeder bucket, and your filter is well tightened down, you should have no trouble. The trick is to keep the bucket well topped up, and use the filter only for fairly clear and well-racked wines.

A powered filter like this is a joy to use – fast, and above all, easy. No more pumping for me!

For those winemakers who abhor DIY, the Buon Vino electric pump and filter from Ritchie Products Ltd costs just under £100 (1995) and does an excellent job of power filtration.

Finally, it has been suggested, though I have not tried it, that if you have home beer-making equipment, put the wine into a five-gallon plastic pressure barrel, pressurise it with carbon dioxide from a gas bottle, and feed it directly to the Vinamat filter, leaving out the hand-pump. Of course, the gas pressure will need to be topped up as the wine level drops in the barrel, and the transfer tube will need to be a tight fit on both the barrel tap and the filter, perhaps secured with small Jubilee clips.

Finally, it should be emphasised that filters are not meant to deal with 'soups' but only with wines which are reasonably clear; the filter's function is to render them brilliant. Harris Filters supply a range of pre-filtration enzymes and finings.

Storage

Many winemakers bottle their wines at this stage, and you may well prefer to do that, so that your bottles can then be placed in racks and be instantly ready for drinking.

My own practice, however, is to keep wine in bulk as long as possible, and only to bottle as required. In this way I find that I obtain a more even quality, that wines are given an adequate maturation period, and that bottlewashing, corking and labelling are reduced to a minimum.

Therefore, in whatever quantity a wine is made, whether one gallon or five gallons, full details are entered in the log book and type and date of making are entered in a luggage label hung on the jar. Mostly wines are stored in 1-gallon jars, which are fitted with safety bungs, so I do not have to worry whether one suddenly starts refermenting (it happens in the best-regulated families!). Wines will stay safe under such bungs for as long as three years.

For daily use they then go into Vinotainer, Brewmaker Wine Dispenser, Adega or similar bag-in-a-box system. The Adega has the advantage of having a polystyrene foam liner, that keeps a chilled wine cool for days. We have two in our kitchen, one for white and one for red. They are filled about once a week and therefore we can draw off a glass whenever we wish, for lunch, supper or during the evening, and the wines keep in perfect condition however long they are left. In this way bottling chores can be virtually eliminated except for special purposes, such as competitions or parties. Decanters can be used in the same way, but in that case the wine needs to be drunk reasonably quickly.

A good system, when breaking into a gallon to fill an ordinary size decanter, is to have 3 one-litre bottles handy as well, and fill those with the remainder of the wine. (Keep those three bottles for that purpose.) They and the decanter will hold exactly one gallon.

Then, as you empty the decanter, refill it from one of the litre bottles. In this way your wine will always be in containers which are full and you will avoid ruining a lot of your wine by oxidation. Until I hit upon this idea I used to tap a 1-gallon jar to fill a decanter. Perhaps the remaining wine would be left and some time later I would discover that it had oxidised or 'gone off'. Using a bag-in-a-box, or a decanter and three 1 litre bottles, avoids this.

Bottling

Whatever system of serving wine you adopt for your own daily purposes you will probably find it useful also to have an adequate supply of bottled wine always to hand in case of 'emergency' – the unexpected visitor, or the impromptu party! Somehow it looks much more 'professional' to be able to draw the cork from an attractively labelled and capsuled bottle of wine rather than pouring from a plain decanter.

A few days before bottling make sure your wine is really stable by moving the jar into a warm place to see if fermentation recommences, also by pouring out a wine-glassful and letting it stand for 24 hours to see if it darkens by oxidation.

If it does re-ferment, the activity will not last long, and you can stabilise the wine by adding 1 g of potassium sorbate and 1 Campden tablet per 4.5 litres (1 gallon).

If the wine oxidises, treat the bulk with Vitamin C (ascorbic acid), which you can buy from your wine supplies shop. Dissolve 10 g in 1 litre and use 25 ml (5 teaspoons) in 4.5 litres (1 gallon) before bottling. You can buy Vitamin C tablets but they are very difficult to dissolve.

You will already have collected your bottles ... it is better to use, if you can, true wine bottles since they show your wine off to better advantage. Be sure that they have been sterilised, with Chempro and rinsed, or sulphite, and allowed to drain, and always use new corks or stoppers (cork, NOT screw, stoppers). Stopper your clean bottles with cotton wool temporarily. There is no need to dry them thoroughly internally. Many wine books warn against using 'damp bottles', but this is only because people have been foolish enough to use bottles containing traces of moisture which may have been in them for a long time, which is not only unhygienic but asking for the wine to be spoilt by the bacteria which are inevitably present. A few drops of sulphite, on the other hand, can do no harm.

Red wines, of course, should be put into dark bottles (except for exhibition or competitive purposes) or they will lose their glorious colour.

Whichever kind of cork you use, soak it briefly in cold boiled water beforehand so soften and swell it, then drive it right home. When using true wine corks, which are cylindrical in shape, a corking machine of some sort is a great help; without one it is difficult to force the cork in far enough. If you have no such tool, push them against a wall to force them home, but this is difficult and the last portion may have to be trimmed off flush. A corker is cheap and greatly simplifies the job.

'Stopper' corks, with plastic projecting caps, are favoured by many, because they are easily withdrawn without a corkscrew and can therefore be used again. They also lend themselves to use with an ornamental capsule, but they do not grip quite so tightly, and are apt to be forced out again by the pressure of the compressed air beneath them. To overcome this, put a length of thick string or pliable wire inside the neck of the bottle, leaving sufficient projecting to be able to grasp it firmly. Insert the cork and drive it home. Then, holding down the stopper with the thumb of the left hand, grasp the string or wire with the right, and pull it out. As it comes out it makes a path which the compressed air follows, thus leaving no pressure within the bottle. Whichever kind of cork you prefer, always try to use new ones (and never one which has been pierced by a corkscrew). If you *have* to use an old one, boil it first.

Some of the most popular stoppers of all nowadays are those made in polythene – winemaking suppliers stock them – which can be used over and over again, and sterilised each time by boiling. They are neat, cheap, and ideal for the home winemaker, and allow bottles to be stored upright.

Finally, finish your bottle off with an appropriate label and coloured capsule of tinfoil or plastic to cover the cork. (It looks better if label and capsule match, and are of a suitable colour for the wine, red label for red wine, yellow for golden, and so on.) The best capsules, I find, are the plastic ones which are just slipped on and then shrunk to tightness in the steam from a boiling kettle. On an ordinary wine bottle the label

All the bottles have been washed and sterilised and the wine is now siphoned into them, leaving about ¾" air space below the bottom of the cork. A small, positive tap (as illustrated) is a great help in controlling the flow – and avoiding a mess.

Useful bottling items . . . rubber mallet and corker, cylindrical and stopper corks, capsules and an applicator, labels and easily applied adhesive (use only on the vertical edges of the label).

should be about a third of the way down the body of the bottle, i.e. the top of it should be about 1½ in. below the shoulder, so that the main line of printing is in the 'optical centre', and looks attractive. The label should be centrally placed between the seams of the bottle and not overlap them, or the appearance is spoilt.

If you have used ordinary cylindrical corks, store your bottles *on their sides*, in a rack or bin if you can, and preferably in a temperature of about 13°C in a place which is free of vibration and not brightly lit. Bottles with stopper corks are safer stored upright, because these are not as secure as full cylindrical corks.

Most white country wines will be at their best about a year to eighteen months after being made but red wines will benefit from longer maturing, up to two or three years. Do not fear that a good, strong country wine will not keep; I have tasted many that have been over 50 years old, and delicious they were. One old lady asked my opinion of some red wine she had in a stone jar, and which her mother had made some 60 years before. Was it safe to drink? It was a deep, ruby red, and absolutely gorgeous, like

Entering up the log.

a vintage port. I finished the tiny glass, and told her so. 'Good,' she said, replacing the stopper. 'You won't want any more, will you?'

Yes, it will keep!

Keeping records

Keep a careful record of all your winemaking activities, with dates of making, racking, bottling etc., and full particulars of recipes. This is a great help in tracking down mistakes and faults, and invaluable if you wish to repeat a particularly successful wine you have formulated yourself. Not to be able to do so for lack of a record would be a disaster! Memory alone plays funny tricks when many wines are involved . . .

Serving your wines

In few subjects is there as much snobbery as in wine appreciation and wine drinking, but happily the spread of our hobby and the widening of wine knowledge and experience that it has brought about has done much to eradicate this.

Admittedly, there are commonly accepted guidelines as to what type of wine to drink with which food, and as a general rule, light, slightly acid white wines go well with shellfish, dry white with fish, cold poultry and white meats, salads and most main course dishes, dry reds with roasts, salads and main courses except fish, and sweeter wines with dessert courses.

But these are *only* guidelines, the consensus of opinion of wine drinkers; they are not *rules*, and as an individual you are free to drink what you like, if you want red wine with fish or sweet wine with meats, that's your choice and privilege. In England, certainly, there is a popular preference for table wines sweeter than the experts would advise. It is all a matter of one's personal taste.

For daily drinking you may well choose to use decanters or one of the modern Vinotainers etc., but if you are serving wine to guests it is usually more effective to present it attractively bottled, labelled and capsuled. There is a great deal of psychology in serving wine, as any wine salesman knows. If you do not respect your own wine you can hardly expect your guests to do so. So *never* present your wine apologetically, with some such remark as 'I *hope* you'll like this...' or 'This is an experiment, really...' thereby putting an immediate doubt into the recipient's mind.

For daily drinking, decanters or refillable dispensers.

No, serve your wine beautifully labelled, and handle the bottle with reverence, preferably making some interesting comment about the age or rarity of that particular wine as you pour it.

Never, never, never serve your guests cloudy or hazy wine. Serve a brilliant wine and use glasses of the right size and of clear or crystal glass, which allow its beauty to be seen and appreciated. Coloured and metal goblets are best avoided because they deprive the drinker of that visual pleasure.

Temperature *is* important. A white wine tastes so much better for being chilled, and a red wine so much better for not being so. White wine can be put in the fridge for up to an hour before it's needed, or placed outside the back door. It should be chilled, but not ice cold. If it's too cold, it will spoil the flavour.

Red wine should be served at room temperature – about 20°C. If your room is between 18° and 22°C, and you have the bottles in it during the day, this will be all right. Take the cork out about an hour before it's wanted, to let the wine breathe. If you have an old wine, this will take only a few minutes or the best goes from it. White wine does not really need to breathe and can be served immediately after opening.

Putting a bottle in a wicker basket might look pretty, but it isn't doing the wine much good. The sediment at the bottom is being continually rocked back and forth without having a chance to settle.

Which brings me to the subject of decanting wine. The reasons for doing this are to aerate the wine, and also to remove the clear wine from any sediment there may be at the bottom of the bottle. If you are drinking a young wine, there is not likely to be much sediment, but there will be with an older wine. Don't throw this away though – use it for cooking.

Remember: show your wines respect, and your guests will do likewise (that is, if the wine is good, which I am sure it will be!).

The malo-lactic fermentation

Occasionally one comes across what is really a third fermentation, the malo-lactic fermentation. This occurs usually after the wine has been bottled, and often as much as a year or more after it was made, but only if the finished wine has not been sulphited. It is something which should be welcomed, when it does occur, for it imparts a very pleasant freshness to a white wine, and does reduce the acidity a little.

Malic acid is the acid to be found in apples, and what happens during the malo-lactic fermentation, as the name indicates, is that a bacterium to be found in all fresh wines (*B. gracile*) sets to work on the malic acid and converts it into lactic acid. This might not seem much of an improvement, but the lactic acid is much *less* acid than malic, and the acidity of the wine is thus reduced, to say nothing of the very pleasant, clean freshness with which this slight fermentation endows the wine, giving it a slight prickle or sparkle.

Occasionally, you can bring about such a fermentation by agitating any yeast deposit and bringing the wine into the warm. Young's Home Brew Ltd now sell 'Prestige' kits which include a sachet of malo-lactic bacteria to ensure this fermentation takes place.

Sparkling wines

A *malo-lactic* fermentation will give you a sparkling wine accidentally, as it were, but it is even more fun to make one deliberately. All you need is a suitable 'must' – apples, pears, gooseberries, rhubarb are all ideal ingredients – a champagne yeast, and not too much sugar (about 2½ lb to 1 gallon, or an SG of 1080–1085, giving a wine of about 10 per cent). Ferment this to dryness, rack twice, mature for about six months, and then bottle in champagne bottles, adding to each 1 level teaspoon of sugar and a little fermenting champagne yeast.

What you are after, of course, is a short in-bottle fermentation which will give the wine that elegant champagne sparkle. This is easy enough to achieve, but the problem is that any such fermentation must inevitably throw a deposit, which will cloud the wine as soon as the cork is removed. Commercially the yeast deposit is removed by 'remuage', i.e. by inverting the bottle in a rack and, by daily twisting, working the yeast down on to the cork. The neck of the bottle is then plunged in a freezing mixture so that the yeast plug is frozen and can be ejected, and the remaining clear wine topped up and recorked and wired. NOT an easy procedure for the amateur.

Much simpler to invest in some of the special stoppers such as the Sparkletops sold by Condessa. These trap the yeast in a hollow plastic stopper, whence it can be vented through a special valve when the bottle is inverted, enabling you to achieve completely clear sparkling wine with ease.

Cork your sparkling wine well and wire the corks, and mature for at least three months. DO NOT MAKE SPARKLING WINE IN ORDINARY BOTTLES: that can be lethal – you are making a glass bomb, because ordinary thin wine bottles will not stand up to the pressures

Neat capsules and labels put a professional touch on your wine. Use a corker, or a corking gun and small mallet, to drive corks right home.

Special wines can be bottled and binned. This wine cellar of mine is held at 13°C (55°F) by a small, thermostat-controlled tubular heater in winter.

73

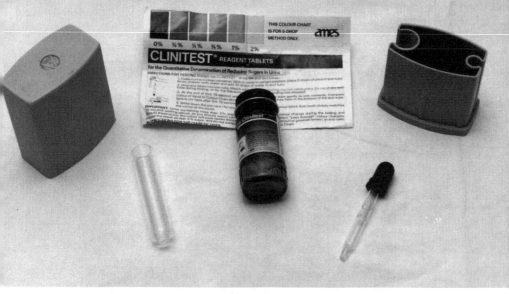

When making sparkling wine you need to know how much residual sugar is in your base wine to be sure of how much sugar you can add with safety, with the yeast, for in-bottle fermentation, thus avoiding explosions. You can measure it by using a Clinitest kit (centre, above) as used by diabetics. This will give you a reading anywhere between 0 and 2%, and for safety the level must never be above (or must be diluted to) 1%. Having discovered the level by Clinitest (full instructions are in the kit) add sugar at the following rates: 0% 15 g/litre (2½ oz/gal); ¼% 12.5 g/litre (2 oz/gal); ½% 10 g/litre (1½ oz/gal); ¾% 7.5 g/litre (1¼ oz/gal); 1% 5 g/litre (¾ oz/gal).

involved, which are equal to those in an ordinary car tyre.

An excellent book on the subject is *Making Sparkling Wines* by John Restall and Don Hebbs (from Nexus Special Interests).

If you wish to make an 'instant' sparkling wine it is quite easy if you are lucky enough to possess one of the carbonating devices now on the market, such as a Sparklets siphon, or a Ritchie Carbonating Kit. Generally the principle is that you select a light white wine, and preferably one that is slightly acid – apple or gooseberry are excellent for the purpose – and chill it in the refrigerator so that it will accept the maximum of carbon dioxide. If the wine is warm the system does not work too well.

The wine is then placed in the siphon or bottle and carbonated by means of a CO_2 bulb or cylinder, according to the instructions with that particular device (some need to be inverted before discharging the gas into them, some do not).

Hey presto! Sparkling wine!

Pasteurisation

Winemakers often ask whether they can stabilise their wines by pasteurisation, i.e. by heat. Certainly this is practised by commercial firms with some cheaper wines but it should be restricted to robust wines, usually reds. The temperature of the wine is raised to 75°C with the bottles stood on a board in hot water, and held there for 20 minutes before driving home sterilised corks.

Winemaking summarised

1.   Extract flavour. Make up must.

2.   Add sugar and yeast and ferment for up to 7 days in a bowl or bucket, closely covered, at about 21°C. (This may be simultaneous with 1.)

3.   Strain off, put into fermentation jar or bottle; fit an airlock. Fill to shoulder; later top up to bottom of neck. Temperature: about 16°C. This fermentation will be much quieter and will proceed for some weeks.

4.   Rack the cleared wine. Repeat this about two months later, and usually, a third time after a further month. By then the wine should be quite stable, with no risk of burst bottles later on.

5.   Bottle when the wine is about six months old. Store bottles, on their sides, preferably in a room of 13°C temperature or below.

Dos and don'ts

Do

- Keep all your equipment spotlessly clean.
- Keep your first ferment closely covered.
- Keep air away from the secondary fermentation.
- Always use fermentation traps.
- Keep all bottles full to within ¾ in. of cork.
- Strain liquor off must slowly and thoroughly.
- Make wines too dry rather than too sweet: sugar them later.
- Use yeast nutrient regularly, and reliable yeast.
- Add sugar by stages. Keep detailed records.

- Rack at least once, and preferably twice or thrice.
- Taste the wine you are making, at intervals.
- Always use new corks or stoppers.
- Keep red wines in dark bottles, or they will lose their colour.

Don't

- Sell or distil your wine.
- Allow a single vinegar fly access to your wine at any stage.
- Use any metal vessel if the wine will be long in contact with it.
- Use any tools or containers of resinous wood.
- Omit to stir a must twice daily.
- Use too much sugar initially.
- Try to speed a fermentation by too high a temperature.
- Be impatient; making wine takes time.
- Let your wine stand on dead yeast or sediment.
- Filter unnecessarily or too soon; most wines will clear of their own accord.
- Put wine in unsterilised bottles or jars.
- Bottle your wine while it is still fermenting.
- Use screw-stoppered bottles.
- Drink too much!

The hydrometer

If the fermentation trap is the winemaker's best friend, it is certainly run a close second by the hydrometer. A hydrometer is by no means essential to the production of good wine, but it is a great help, particularly if you are aiming at consistent results. No one who has used one intelligently would willingly be without one. It is as well, however, to keep things in perspective, and to appreciate that a hydrometer is meant to be used only as a general guide, and cannot be one hundred per cent accurate in the estimation of final alcohol content. So it is foolish to become a slave to it, and to try to calculate things to the second place of decimals!

Equally, do not be overawed by it, for it is a useful tool. Many winemakers seem to fight shy of it, but in principle it is quite a simple device; by means of it you can:

(a)   determine how much sugar there is in any natural juice or must;

(b)   determine how much sugar to add to a juice to produce a wine of the desired strength;

(c)   keep a check on the process of a ferment; and
(d)   calculate the strength of the finished wine.

The word hydrometer means 'water-measurer', but in this instance it would be more accurate to call it a saccharometer, or 'sugar-measurer', for the basic purpose of the instrument is to discover how much sugar there is in the must or wine. Fermentation, as has been explained, involves the conversion by yeast of sugar into alcohol and carbon dioxide. If, therefore, we can discover how much sugar is used up during the whole course of a ferment, we can calculate exactly how much alcohol has been produced, how strong the wine is.

The more sugar there is in a liquid, the thicker or denser it will become, or the greater its *gravity* will be. The better, too, it will support anything floating in it; the hydrometer makes use of this principle. To measure different gravities, we naturally need a scale of some sort, and an obvious and convenient standard from which to start is that of water. Water is therefore given the arbitrary gravity of 1.000, other liquids are compared specifically with this, and the resultant figures are said to be their *specific gravities*.

Thus liquids heavier than water (or, in our case, containing more sugar) may have *specific gravities* such as 1.050, 1.120 or 1.117 degrees. When talking of gravities, however, we omit the first '1' and the decimal

Below: Several types of winemaking and brewing hydrometers. Saccharometer, or sugar measurer, would be a more accurate description.

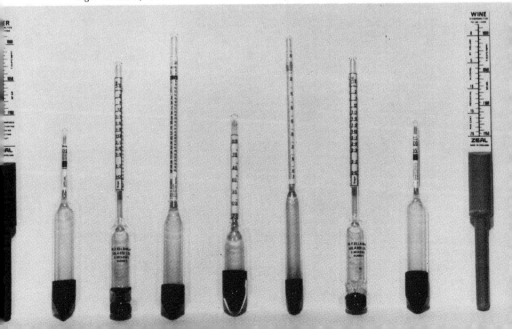

point. Therefore the *specific* gravities are quoted exactly as the same as *gravities* of 50, 120 and 117 respectively. Gravities are the same as degrees Gay Lussac (deg GL).

For winemaking you will need hydrometers, or perhaps one hydrometer, covering the range 1.000 to 1.160 and it is often useful to be able to go several degrees below the 1.000.

Several firms now produce hydrometers made specially for winemakers, some of which even indicate when it is safe to bottle – and you will have no difficulty obtaining one from your local wine-making shop.

A hydrometer is a glass tube (with a bulbous lower end) containing the scale, and it is weighted at the bottom so that it will float upright in a liquid. The reading is taken where the level of the main surface of the liquid would cut the scale.

The thinner the liquid (the less its gravity) the deeper the hydrometer will sink in it; the denser the liquid (the greater its gravity) the higher

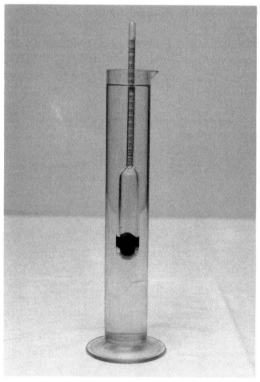

Reading the hydrometer.

the hydrometer will float, and the more of the scale will protrude above the surface.

Therefore the scale of figures in the hydrometer is 'upside down', the smallest being at the top and the largest at the bottom. In water, of course, the hydrometer will float with the 1.000 mark level with the surface; as you add sugar so the hydrometer will rise in the liquid. If, on the other hand, you add instead to the water a liquid *lighter* than water – alcohol, for instance – the hydrometer will sink *below* 1.000. So really dry wines may be as low as 995 or even less.

To use your hydrometer, pour some of the juice or syrup to be measured into a hydrometer jar, or any transparent container that gives sufficient depth and ample side clearance. Spin the hydrometer to get rid of any air bubbles clinging to its sides, which can seriously affect the reading. When the hydrometer is still, take the reading, with the eye at surface level.

Note that the hydrometers are designed to be read when the liquid is at 15°C, and, strictly speaking, if it is at any other temperature, you should allow for it as shown in the following table. Omit the 'decimal point' of the specific gravity and make the correction to the last of its four figures. Example: A hydrometer reading of 1140 at 30°C should be corrected at 1143.4.

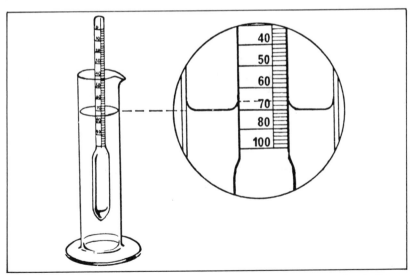

With the eye at the level of the surface of the liquid, the correct reading is 70, and NOT 66.

Temperature Dec C/Deg F		Correction	Temperature Deg C/Deg F		Correction
11	50	Subtract 0.6	27	77	Add 2
15	59	Correct	30	86	Add 3.4
20	68	Add 0.9	35	95	Add 5
			161	104	Add 6.8

When you have measured the specific gravity of your juice or must, you can tell from the following tables firstly how much sugar it contains, and, secondly, how much alcohol (in terms of the percentage of alcohol by volume) it is likely to produce, i.e. you can assess its potential alcoholic strength. You can thus work out how much sugar to add to produce a wine of the strength you want. This, remember, on the assumption that the wine ferments right out, and that all the sugar is used up.

There may be some obscuration, or unavoidable inaccuracy, at either end of the scale, caused by solids initially, and alcohol finally, but these figures give a practical working basis, and a deliberately conservative estimate of potential alcohol.

To avoid having an unduly complicated table, we have given two for SG/sugar/alchol, one metric, one imperial.

Let us assume that you wish to make a wine using a diluted fruit juice. Having extracted the fruit juice and diluted it with water as required, take the SG of it. Let us assume that you obtain a reading on the hydrometer of 1.040. This means, if you look at the tables for a moment, that there is already 1 lb 1 oz (480 g) of sugar present in the natural juice and that if you fermented it you would finish up with a dry wine of 5 per cent alcohol by volume. This would probably not keep (under 10 per cent it cannot be guaranteed).

So now you have to decide how strong a wine you wish to make. You can of course make a weak wine of, say 5 per cent, but it would have to be drunk young, and most winemakers prefer to make table wines, which are usually of about 10–12 per cent alcohol, or stronger wines of up to 17 per cent. For wines above the latter strength, say for drinking *after* a meal, you must resort to fortification.

Say you decide to make a wine of 12 per cent alcohol. The table shows that you will require an initial SG of 1090, or a sugar content in the gallon of 2 lb 6 oz (metric 1065 g). You already have 1 lb 1 oz (480 g) so that you will need to add 1 lb 5 oz (585 g) of sugar and make the quantity

up to 1 gallon with more juice *of the same dilution as the measured portion.*
Alternatively, if you wish to add sugar to a gallon of diluted juice
which has an SG of 1040 and arrive at an SG of 1090 you need to obtain
a further 50 degrees of gravity. This is easily done if you remember that
2 ¼ oz (56 g) of sugar will raise the SG of 1 gallon by 0.005 (5 degrees of
gravity). So you need about 1 lb 6 ½ oz (630 g) of sugar.

SG	Potential per cent alcohol by volume	Amount of sugar in the gallon		Amount of sugar added to the gallon		Volume of 1 gallon with sugar added	
		lb	oz	lb	oz	gal	fl oz
1010	0.9		2		2 ½	1	1
1015	1.6		4		5	1	3
1020	2.3		7		8	1	5
1025	3.0		9		10	1	7
1030	3.7		12		13	1	8
1035	4.4		15	1	0	1	10
1040	5.1	1	1	1	2	1	11
1045	5.8	1	3	1	4	1	13
1050	6.5	1	5	1	7	1	14
1055	7.2	1	7	1	9	1	16
1060	7.8	1	9	1	11	1	17
1065	8.6	1	11	1	14	1	19
1070	9.2	1	13	2	1	1	20
1075	9.9	1	15	2	4	1	22
1080	10.6	2	1	2	6	1	23
1085	11.3	2	4	2	9	1	25
1090	12.0	2	6	2	12	1	27
1095	12.7	2	8	2	15	1	28
1100	13.4	2	10	3	2	1	30
1105	14.1	2	12	3	5	1	32
1110	14.9	2	14	3	8	1	33
1115	15.6	3	0	3	11	1	35
1120	16.3	3	2	3	14	1	37
1125	17.0	3	4	4	1	1	38
1130	17.7	3	6	4	4	1	40
1135	18.4	3	8	4	7	1	42

SG	Potential per cent alcohol by volume	Grammes of sugar in 4.5 litres	Grammes of sugar added to 4.5 litres	Vol in mls of 4.5 litres with sugar added
1010	0.9	55	70	4530
1015	1.6	125	140	4590
1020	2.3	195	210	4650
1025	3.0	265	280	4710
1030	3.7	320	350	4740
1035	4.4	410	420	4780
1040	5.1	480	490	4810
1045	5.8	535	560	4850
1050	6.5	590	630	4900
1055	7.2	645	700	4960
1060	7.8	705	770	4990
1065	8.6	760	840	5040
1070	9.2	815	910	5070
1075	9.9	870	980	5130
1080	10.6	930	1050	5160
1085	11.3	1010	1120	5220
1090	12.0	1065	1200	5280
1095	12.7	1125	1275	5300
1100	13.4	1180	1355	5350
1105	14.1	1235	1445	5410
1110	14.9	1290	1535	5440
1115	15.6	1345	1625	5500
1120	16.3	1400	1715	5560
1125	17.0	1455	1805	5590
1130	17.7	1510	1900	5640
1135	18.4	1565	1995	5700

Going back to our 1 gallon ... You can, of course, add all the sugar at the outset, as long as you ensure that it is thoroughly dissolved, and, if you then check with your hydrometer, the SG should be in the region of 1090. Add a little of the sugar at a time to be on the safe side, testing as you go.

You then add your yeast nutrient and ferment in the usual manner.

As the ferment proceeds the SG of the liquor will drop, rapidly at first, and then more slowly, and you can gain a good idea of its progress by noting the rate of drop. As it nears the 1.000 mark it will be very slow indeed. It may go well below 1.000 because of the presence of alcohol, in which case congratulate yourself upon having produced a really dry wine!

To calculate the final strength of the wine, write down (omitting the decimal point) the SG at the start of the ferment (i.e. after the sugar was added). Subtract from it the final SG, and divide the answer by 7.36; that is the percentage of alcohol by volume of your wine.

Example:	Starting SG	1090
	Final SG	995
	Drop	95

95 ÷ 7.36 = 12.9 per cent alcohol by vol.
Multiplied by 7-4ths = 22.5 deg. proof.

(To turn degrees proof into per cent alcohol by volume, one reverses the procedure, of course.)

It is always good practice in winemaking to add the sugar by stages, but winemakers are often puzzled as to how they can do this, yet still use their hydrometer to obtain the information they want as to their wine's strength. It is easy enough if one bears in mind all the time that the principal factor with which one is concerned in calculating the final strength of the wine is the *total drop* in specific gravity. The sugar can therefore be added a few ounces at a time *as long as you keep a record of the number of degrees drop between successive additions.* Then add up the various drops and this is the figure to be divided by 7.36 in the usual way. This will, in normal cases, give an approximate result which will be accurate enough for the average winemaker, but where large quantities of syrup are added it can be seriously adrift because it takes no account of the volumes involved. When you have worked out what percentage of alcohol you have obtained by the first drop, you then proceed to add sugar or syrup. This produces more alcohol, but its bulk also dilutes the alcohol you have already produced, so you must modify the calculation already done. Similarly the drop from the second lot of sugar must be modified, and so on.

Suppose you start with an SG of 1100 and, after three or four days, strain into a one-gallon jar and obtain 5 pints of liquid. Some time subsequently the SG is found to be 1000, i.e. a drop of 100. Since a gallon is required you 'top up' these 5 pints, bring them to 7½ pints with an SG of 1010. After another period the SG drops again to 1005, so once more

83

you top up with syrup or sugar to obtain a full 8 pints with an SG of 1010. The SG finally drops to 1005.

Using the rough-and-ready calculation above gives a total drop of 100 + 5 + 5 = 110. This you divide by 7.36, giving a result of 15 per cent alcohol by volume.

But the correct calculation would be:

First drop: 100.

This must be modified into:

$$100 \times \frac{5 \text{ (the number of pints before topping up)}}{7\frac{1}{2} \text{ (the number of pints after topping up)}}$$

$$= 100 \times \frac{2}{3} = 66.6$$

Second drop: 5.

Added to modified first drop = 66.6 + 5 = 71.6. This again must be modified due to the second addition of sugar, as follows:

$$71.6 \times \frac{7\frac{1}{2}}{8} = 67$$

Final drop: 5.

To this 67 is added the final drop of 5, giving a total effective drop of 67 + 5 = 72. This represents just under 10 per cent alcohol by volume, as against 15 per cent by the crude method.

Admittedly this is a deliberately exaggerated case and is not common winemaking practice, but it does illustrate the mathematical point.

A good general rule is that a really dry wine will often need a starting specific gravity of about 1.085, a medium sweet wine one of about 1.100, and a really sweet wine one of up to 1.125.

You can achieve these results quite simply by always using 1 kilo of sugar *in* the gallon (a convenient, ready-packed quantity!) or 1120 gm (2½ lb) *to* the gallon. This will always produce dry wines, which can then be sweetened to taste finally by the cautious addition of one, or two, drops of Sweetex, Canderel tablets, or some such non-fermentable sweetener. The only caveat I would enter is that if you wish to make the heavier-bodied social or dessert wines the fruit content will have to be increased accordingly, and with dessert wines it will be necessary to practise 'feeding' the ferment with 4-oz doses of sugar as it nears its end.

But it is certainly better to use too little sugar initially than too much; a dry wine can always be sweetened; an oversweet wine is hard to redeem. Make your wines dry, and sweeten them to taste when finished.

Another useful point to note is that if you wish to *reduce* the gravity of a liquid, it can be done by dilution. The addition of an equal quantity of water, for instance, will reduce the gravity by half.

Pearson square

Sometimes you will want to fortify a wine (raise its alcoholic content by adding spirit) and, since spirit is expensive, you will need to calculate exactly how much to add to achieve the desired result. Do so by means of the Pearson Square (or St Andrew's Cross), but note that all measures must be of the same sort, i.e. per cent alcohol by volume or (USA) degrees proof; do not mix them.

Here is the Pearson Square:

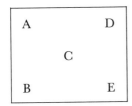

A = alcohol content of spirit to be added
B = present alcohol content of wine
C = desired alcohol content
D = difference between B and C
E = difference between C and A

The proportion D to E is the proportion of spirit to wine to achieve the desired strength.

If you are blending two wines of known strength and wish to know the final strength, the formula is:

$$\frac{(A \times B) + (C \times D)}{A + C} \text{ where:}$$

A = No. of parts of 1st wine
B = Strength of 1st wine
C = No. of parts of 2nd wine
D = Strength of 2nd wine

85

Thus, if you blend two parts of a wine of 15 per cent with three parts of a wine of 10 per cent the result will be:

$$\frac{(2 \times 15) + (3 \times 10)}{2 + 3} = \frac{60}{5} = 12$$

or a wine of 12 per cent.

The Pearson Square is particularly useful if you are using your own wine, plus some Polish Spirit and some of the excellent flavourings now on the market to make liqueurs. Flavourings are also obtainable to produce liqueurs at home – Cherry Brandy, Curacao, Green and Yellow Convent, Kirsch, Eau-de-Vie, Juniper Gin etc., etc. With liqueurs, of course, some fortification with brandy or vodka is to be recommended, to obtain the strength required (liqueurs are really sweetened spirits). Some economy can be effected by using a proportion of strong wine in place of a third of the amount of spirit recommended by the suppliers. This topic is covered in *Making Wines Like Those You Buy* by Acton & Duncan (Nexus Special Interests).

It is also possible to make French and Italian vermouth and one firm in particular, Condessa, sells excellent blended herbs to convert your wines to vermouth. Various branded Vermouth Kits are also on sale.

The new Liqueur Wine and Spirit Wine kits reach an alcohol content of 20% abv or more, and open up many exciting possibilities for experimentation in this field.

Wine in quantity

Sooner or later, most winemakers are not content to make just one gallon of their favourite wines; their thoughts turn to the idea of making them in larger quantities, say 4½, 5 or 6 gallons, or even more.

Many winemakers make 20 or 30 gallons of their favourite wine each year (and this 'bulk' method has much to commend it), but many are nervous of attempting, say, five gallons of one wine. But it is a fact that five gallons is much less liable to 'go wrong' than one, if ordinary precautions are observed.

And consider the advantages . . . wine seems to ferment better in bulk (in small quantities it is like a plant in too small a pot!); the large bulk means that it is less subject to violent temperature fluctuations; it is very little more trouble to make five gallons than to make one (and it lasts nearly twice as long!). Certainly, if you have a good stock of wine, bolstered by one or two wines made in quantity, there is less temptation to drink wine which is immature, and you can still do your experimental single gallons. The advent of wine kits, which make it easy to produce five gallons at a time, has proved the truth of this philosophy that I have been preaching for the last 40 years.

By making a few wines in bulk you can have as much wine to drink as you wish, every day ... a satisfying thought.

Modern fermenting and storage vessels.

Equipment for winemaking on a larger scale: various big fermenters.

Below: (left) A large fermenting bucket with fermentation trap, heater, and tap, (right) the excellent Bruheat boiler, with thermostatically controlled element. It can handle five gallons.

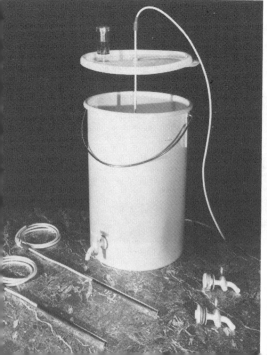

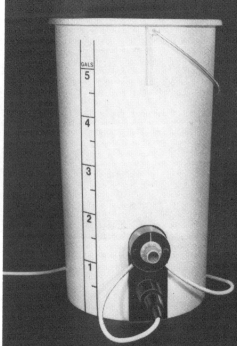

The way to set about it is to choose one or two ingredients which are readily available, or very cheap, and which can be relied upon to give you a wine of reasonable quality for your *vin ordinaire*, both red and white.

I personally have settled for apple for the white (from which a whole range of wines can be produced), and elderberry or grape juice concentrate for the red.

The apple I make on the principle of 12 lb of mixed apples to 1 gallon of water, which gives 1½ gallons of 'juice'. (Metric: 5 kilos apples

Arthur Tucker gets busy with the 'scratcher', or crusher. Apple pulp falls into the bin below.

89

to 5 litres.) Twelve pounds of apples fill a plastic bucket (an easy measure) and are run through a crusher, the resultant 'purée' falling into an 11 gallon bin.

From here it is ladled into the basket of my press and pressing starts. The juice runs out through a fine sieve into one-gallon jars, so that it is automatically measured. I find that 12 lb of apples almost always give ½ a gallon of juice, and I add water at the rate of 2 of water to 1 of juice.

This all goes into a brew-bin and for each gallon I add 1 kilo sugar

Whilst I set to with the press.

Apple wine production line 'on stream'!

and 150 ml of white grape concentrate, 1 level teaspoon citric acid and the usual nutrients.

Then stir well to dissolve all the sugar before pouring all the must into a plastic fermenter, under an airlock, for the main fermentation – and the wine is made. A fermentation lock is fitted in place of the tap, of course.

Apples are usually readily obtained free in our area and we use a couple of hundredweight each year.

For many years my bulk house red wine was made from imported dried bilberries, one of the finest ingredients for many 'country' red wines. Unhappily, these have now become so expensive that they have disappeared from the market. Bottled berries are still imported, but these are usually too costly for use in bulk. Fresh bilberries can be picked from the wild, but who has the fortitude to pick enough for five or ten gallons of wine?

The modern equivalent, when it comes to quality, is to make up one or more of the grape juice kits designed to produce one or five gallons of wine. There are numerous such kits on the market, and they are either wholly grape juice concentrate or grape juice concentrate and added sugar. They can be bought in a number of specific grape varieties, such as Cabernet Sauvignon, Merlot, and Malbec, and produce excellent table wines for an average of 80p a bottle (1995). There are many cheaper kits that are made from unspecified grapes, or from blends of fruit juices and dried fruits etc. that produce perfectly satisfactory wines.

If economy is paramount, or you particularly enjoy the challenge, and the ultimate pride and joy of making wines from fresh ingredients, then I suggest you use either the Dried elderberry recipe for February, or if fresh or frozen elderberries are available, the Elderberry and runner bean wine recipe given for September.

Both these recipes can be scaled up proportionately to make five or ten gallons. If you are short of runner beans, increase the grape concentrate to compensate. Simmer the elderberries in water for 15 minutes beforehand. This reduces the amount of tannin extracted, giving a fruitier wine that can be drunk younger.

For making wines in quantity an ideal brewing boiler is the Bruheat, marketed by Ritchie Products, or that sold by Thorne Electrim, or any gas or electric boiler holding, say, 5 gallons. All we need it for in winemaking, of course, is boiling up large quantities of liquid but these have the added advantage that they are equipped with a thermostat, most useful in holding a beer mash at a critical temperature when brewing beer. A large brewing bin, 11-gallon size, is useful, so is a fruit crusher to avoid having to cut up large quantities of fruit. A press you can do without at a pinch, and use pectin-destroying enzyme to break down the fruit instead. A large wooden paddle is useful for stirring, so is a 'plonker' for pushing down the cap of fruit during mashing. Both these are easily made from broom handles and squares of oak. A small trolley for moving heavy containers and a length of hose which can be fixed to your taps for rinsing them are also very useful.

It is still possible occasionally to obtain from off-licences and restaurants the 'ex-wine fives', (5 gallon polypins or cubitainers), collapsible plastic containers housed in a rigid cardboard box. Rinse and sulphite them well, and they are suitable for winemaking and short-term wine storage. Squeeze the tap out of its collar, and the polypin will then accept a standard demijohn bung. Or ask your supplier for a Vina 'Drafty' container. As these plastic containers are slightly porous, they are not suitable for long storage of wines to mature; they will slowly oxidise the wines.

Other containers for fermenting and storage? Carboys: fragile, but OK if they are kept in their metal or plastic protective baskets. Make sure they are thoroughly cleaned before you use them, as they may have contained acids. If it's urgent, you can use a large plastic bag supported by a cardboard carton, but this can only be a short-term solution; get the wine must into a permanent container(s) as soon as possible. You can't fit an airlock, so use an elastic band loosely fitted. Always check that any plastic you use is food grade, and you will avoid contaminating your wine with the plasticisers used in making cheap containers.

All in all, I still prefer glass for long-term storage, and use it whenever possible. One-gallon jars are *always* safe!

My rule of thumb on storage, therefore, is: use glassware or stoneware whenever available; use plastic only if unavoidable, and test it before you trust it!

Casks

"But what about casks?" I can hear you saying. If you have the time to look after them and the wine they contain (and can get them), they are excellent; they are safe, easy to handle, long lasting and do impart 'character' to a wine, but unfortunately they are increasingly difficult to obtain. Optimum sizes for home use are probably the 4½ gallon and 6 gallon sizes, a 3 gallon being rather too small and a 9 gallon heavy to move. Paradoxically, the larger a cask is the cheaper it is proportionally.

A few golden rules: avoid like the plague casks which smell of vinegar. Keep your cask on a stand or stillage, so that the centre bottom

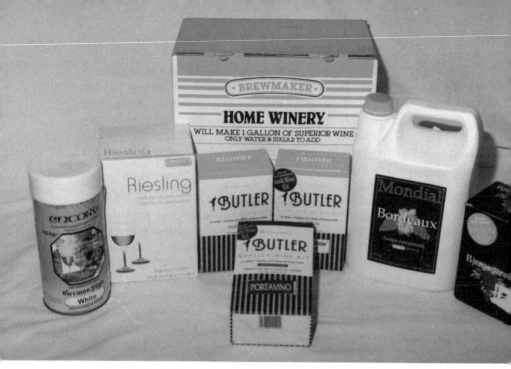

A few of the many reliable kits currently on sale.

stave is not supporting all the weight; *always keep casks FULL* (most important), topping them up regularly; refill a cask as soon as it is emptied; avoid the use of taps (which always drip and leak and harbour bacteria) and siphon wine out through the bung hole. Use always oak casks, wine casks if possible (beer 'barrels' are thicker). Siphon wine into 1-gallon jars or bottles for drinking and refill cask. Normally keep separate casks for white and red wines.

To prepare new casks   Wash out the cask with warm water, making sure there are no wood shavings, dust, or cobwebs inside. Most casks for home brewing are 5-gallon size, so two gallons of hot water for washing will be sufficient. Put the bung in the cask, and rock the cask from side to side, turning it as you go; this should remove any debris from the inside. Then empty the water out through the bunghole.

Mix 8 oz of common salt in two pints of hot water, mix well, and pour it into the cask. Fill the cask with hot water – about 150°F. Do not use boiling water, as this might crack the staves. Leave for five or six days, then empty out, and rinse the cask well with fresh water until no trace of salt can be tasted in the rinsing water. Then drain the cask.

After this treatment, the cask can be treated with a pint of 10% solution of sodium metabisulphite. Swirl it round the cask, and empty it away, if the cask is to be used at once. If not, leave the solution in the cask and replace the bung. The sulphur dioxide fumes will keep the cask fresh and free from bacteria for four or five weeks, after which time the solution will have to be replaced with fresh.

To sterilise secondhand casks   The same treatment can be used. If there is a deposit in the cask, this can usually be removed by placing a 3 ft length of heavy chain in the cask (secure the end with a length of string through the bung-hole), fill the cask with hot water, and roll it around until all the deposits are loosened. Then empty it, and give the cask the salt treatment.

Musty or stagnant smelling casks   Rinse out the cask with a gallon of boiling water; keep this moving in the cask, to prevent cracking. Then empty the cask. You can then steam the cask. Turn the cask upside down on the sink, and run a pipe from this to a pressure cooker. Remove the pressure relief valve, and insert the pipe. Steam for about twenty minutes; you may see dirt dripping from the bung-hole. After this, rinse well with hot water, and treat with salt as above.

Storage   Wash thoroughly as soon as emptied, removing all surface deposit with chain, sterilise with sulphite solution. Some of this (say ½ gallon for a 4½ or 6 gallon cask) should be left in the bunged up cask. Store cask on end; invert at intervals; renew solution every month or so.

Improving your wines by blending

Do not fall into the error of assuming that once a wine is made, that is how it must be drunk, and that nothing can be done to improve it. Many wines fall just short of excellence because some minor fault has gone uncorrected.

A lack of balance – too much or too little acidity, sweetness, flavour, body or bouquet – can often be remedied, and one simple method (and enjoyable, since it involves a good deal of tasting!) is blending, or mixing two or more wines to counterbalance their characteristics, a bland one with a rough one, an under-acid one with an over-acid one, and so on.

You can blend to balance excess against deficiency in:

- Body/thinness
- Taste/lack of flavour
- Sweetness/dryness

- Acidity
- Blandness or insipidity/tannic harshness
- Bouquet
- Colour

The golden rules in blending are:

(a)   Always blend wines which are 'sympathetic' or compatible (red with red, white with white, etc.).

(b)   Blend small measured samples first to establish proportions required when blending in bulk.

(c)   Never blend diseased or really bad wines in the hope of improving them. Instead of one bad wine and one good you will have two bad!

(d)   Always expect the blended wine to referment, however stable the individual wines were. The new fermentation will be quite brief, possibly two or three days, while the two wines 'marry'.

Always take a sample of your wine before bottling or use to see if any improvement can be made by some minor adjustment.

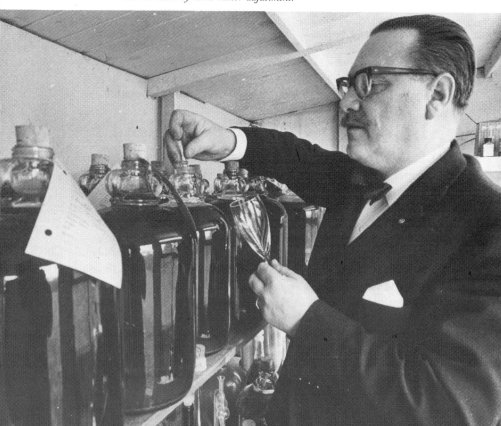

(e)   Remember that, as a winemaker (unlike a young Lothario) it will often pay you to 'marry' your mistakes!

Chamber of horrors!

It may be you have no wines suitable for blending but still have wines that you wish to improve, or wines which have minor faults.

While something must be said about faults and diseases of wine, it should be emphasised at once that several of these disasters which can befall your wines are rarely encountered. Observance of commonsense precautions will ensure that your wines are sound, and you may never need to refer to these particular pages. I hope you do not! – but 'just in case' there are listed here some of the disasters most probable to be encountered.

Acetification

. . . or formation of vinegar. This will normally only occur in conditions of extremely bad storage, and in the presence of air. Therefore keep your bottles full. If it is noticed in the early stages – there is a very slight smell of vinegar and an acid taste – it can probably be halted by adding one Campden tablet per gallon, waiting 24 hours, and then introducing a vigorously fermenting fresh yeast. In the later stages the smell of vinegar will be pronounced, and indeed what you have now *is* wine vinegar. Remedy: use it for cooking or pour it down the drain!

Sometimes a wine will smell vinegary but not taste acid, and this is the effect of ethyl acetate, produced by wild yeast present on the fruit. Prevent this by adding one Campden tablet per gallon 24 hours before your chosen yeast.

Over-sweetness

The bugbear of the beginner. It can be avoided by not using too much sugar initially and always using a nutrient (see pages 32 to 36). Remedy: blend the wine with one from similar ingredients which is over dry, or with dry rhubarb wine, which will take up its flavour. See also 'Low Alcohol Content'. Alternatively, try to get it to ferment further, as you would a 'stuck' wine. Four methods:

(a)   Add nutrient, particularly Vitamin B_1. Stir; place in warm place. Add fresh vigorous yeast.

(b)   Put on to lees of a must which has fermented vigorously and just been racked.

(c)   Add a cupful of vigorously fermenting must.

(d)   Finally, adopt the 'doubling-up' method with a fresh yeast starter bottle.

Not enough zest

Flatness or insipidity is due to a lack of tannin. Add grape tannin, or soak apple peel or oak leaves in wine, or add a small quantity of strong tea (up to 1 tablespoon per gallon).

Too harsh

Add a trace of glycerine or remove some tannin by adding gelatine finings (1 teaspoon in a little warm water).

Too much acidity

Mask with glycerine (up to 5 per cent, or 1 pint to 2½ gallons) or sugar, if only slight. Or reduce with *potassium carbonate*, which leaves no sediment and does not impair flavour, 9 oz made up to 1 pint of solution (½ fl oz reduces acidity of 1 gallon by 1 ppt); or with *chalk, calcium carbonate*: ¼ oz (7 g) reduces acidity of 1 gallon by 1.6 ppt. Or you can buy proprietary reducing solutions. In the case of some strong wines you can reduce acidity by simple dilution.

Too little acidity

Add citric acid. ¼ oz (7 g) raises acidity of 1 gallon by 1 ppt.

Not enough body

(a)   Add grape concentrate, or

(b)   add glycerine, but not too much or wine will taste 'hot', or

(c)   add the juice of a few bananas, and

(d)   make a note to use more fruit next time!

Naturally thin wines, such as plum, can be improved by adding up to 1 lb of wheat, barley or maize to the gallon when making. Regularly

using a Campden tablet per gallon in the 'must' 24 hours before adding
the yeast will also improve the wine by putting into it a little glycerine.
Thinness in a finished wine can also be overcome by judicious blending
with one of considerably more body. Banana wine and robust grain wines
are excellent for this purpose, since they usually have a good body.

Poor bouquet

Usually caused by too rapid a fermentation, poor ingredients, or the use
of excessive nutrient. Keep up the acid level; use a little succinic, malic
and lactic acid as well as citric. Add aromatic substances – rosepetals,
elderflower, raspberry, etc., or blend in a cupful of wine made from them.

Too much colour

See charcoal treatment under 'Taints and smells'.

Poor colour

To improve reds, add a cupful of elderberry to any red wine, or, Gervin
brand Red Grape Colour. This is mainly anthocyanins, and has no known
side effects; as E163 it is fully approved for food use. NB: over-sulphiting
may reduce or change the colour of your wine or must, but this is usually
only temporary. The tip of a teaspoon of salt per gallon will help to fix the
colour of a red wine.

Lightening white wines

Add 2 tablespoons dried milk to the gallon. Rack off two days later. This
works wonderfully well but not on an oxidised white wine.

Oxidation

Add the oxidised wine to a strongly fermenting and compatible wine and
the excess acetaldehyde is caught up in the fermentation process and
reduced to alcohol with the aldehyde of the fermenting must.

Hazes

Pectin   Treat with Pectinol or Pektolase as directed. 1 teaspoon in ½ pint
wine, kept warm for 4 hours. Then strain into bulk of wine. (See 'Clearing'.)   99

Starch   Treat with Fungal Amylase 2209 (10 per cent). ½ teaspoon to 5 gallons. (See 'Clearing'.)

Protein   Fine with Bentonite, Liquid Chitin (Winecleer, etc.) at ½ fl oz per gallon, or add 'banana gravy'. Filter if necessary. (See 'Clearing'.)

Coloured hazes   Usually the result of metallic contamination, copper, zinc, or iron being the usual causes. They may appear after a sudden drop in temperature renders the solutes less soluble. Add a little citric acid; this often works. (If still hazy after fining – filter.)

Taints and smells

Not always readily identifiable; they can be caused by damaged fruit, bacterial action, tainted plastic containers, bad casks, or proximity of wine to strong smell (onion, paraffin, etc.). They can occasionally be removed by charcoal treatment but it is necessary to experiment to discover how much charcoal is needed. Add a small quantity to a measured quantity of wine, stir two or three times during the first 24 hours. Allow to settle. Leave a further day, then rack, and filter to remove particles of charcoal. Some of the flavour and colour may also be removed. If dose is satisfactory treat the bulk of wine proportionately. If it is not decrease or increase it to achieve the desired result.

'Mousey' wine

A horrible odour of 'mice' instantly detected if a drop is rubbed on the palm of the hand and smelt. It is that of acetamide, produced by spoilage bacteria. You can try charcoal – 1 tablespoon to the gallon. Shake occasionally. When the smell has disappeared – together, probably, with the colour and flavour! – rack and filter. At least you have saved the alcohol. Then blend with a bottle of grape juice or apple juice to make a drinkable plonk. I prefer to throw the lot away and sterilise everything in sight!

Flowers of wine

Powdery, whitish flecks appear on the surface of the wine and if left unchallenged will rapidly increase and will turn your wine first into carbon dioxide and then to water. It is caused by an organism like yeast, mycoderma, an aerobic film yeast, *Candida mycoderma*, which consumes alcohol, and is usually the result of admitting too much air to the fermenting vessel. Remedy: remove as much of the surface flecks as possible, filter through kitchen paper towel or filter papers, introduce some vigorous fresh yeast, and fill the fermenting bottle as full as possible to exclude all air. If fermentation is complete before it occurs, filter and add Campden tablet. If a substantial film has been formed there is no remedy.

Ropiness

The wine takes on a repellent, oily appearance, and pours very slowly, like treacle, but the taste is unaffected. The wine will look rather like the raw white of an egg and in it will appear rope-like coils – hence the name. This is the work of the lactic acid bacterium. Remedy: whip the wine into a froth in a polythene bucket, add two crushed Campden tablets per gallon and filter.

Too dry

If for immediate drinking sweeten wine in decanter or jug; usually a dessert-spoon sugar will suffice. *If for storage or show* add sugar syrup and 50 ppm sulphite *or* sweeten with lactose, glycerine, Sorbitol, Hermesetas or Sweetex but be careful not to overdo it. (These are non-fermentable.)

Medicinal flavour

The result of insufficient acid in the must. If the fault is but slight the addition of a little citric acid to the finished wine may help, but if the flavour is pronounced little can be done.

Mustiness

Usually caused by standing overlong on baker's yeast or by musty casks.

Low alcohol content

Usually allied to over-sweetness. If it is the result of a fermentation having ceased prematurely, adding fresh yeast direct will rarely succeed, since it will be inhibited by the alcohol present. Remedy: make up half-a-pint of fresh juice with 1 oz of sugar and some fresh yeast and nutrient as a 'starter'. When it is fermenting vigorously add an equal quantity of the low-alcohol wine. When all is fermenting well, again add an equal quantity of the wine, and continue the process until the whole is fermenting once more. Adding nutrient to the bulk and keeping at 21°C will help.

Metallic flavour

Sometimes encountered when wines have been made with tinned fruit, juice, or concentrate, or when ferrous metals have been allowed prolonged contact with the wine. Remedy: avoid 'unsafe' metals.

Failure to clear

Usually the result of over-boiling the ingredients (see 'Hazes') or of hastening unduly the initial straining, which should be both slow and thorough. Remedy: move wine into cold place for two or three weeks and see if it clears. If not, try filtering or Bentonite (see page 55) or using a good wine finings, such as Winecleer. If these fail, try pouring into the top quarter of the bottle some *clear* wine of the same variety. This will often carry down the suspended solids. Isinglass or gelatine as finings are tricky, and not recommended for the beginner.

Grow your own grapes

"But surely you can't ripen grapes out of doors in this country?" This, with variations, is the common incredulous reaction one gets each time the subject of outdoor vine-growing is mentioned to the average Englishman.

Vines, so the popular belief runs, are delicate, temperamental things, hard to propagate, complicated to prune, and suitable really only for greenhouse culture, and even then only by an expert viticulturist. And even if one succeeds in growing some vines, declare the pessimists, in our climate it will be impossible to ripen the crop.

These fallacies are widely believed, even among amateur wine-makers, yet are the opposite of the truth.

Vines *can* be grown successfully in the southern half of England, and in a reasonably good summer the grapes can be ripened (a really wet one admittedly produces problems). And when we get one of our really hot summers, as we do occasionally, the owner of a vine is a happy man indeed.

Vines were grown in southern Britain by the Romans (so this is no new idea!) and today there are over 300 small vineyards where experiments are once more being made in order to accumulate indigenous experience again. In Hampshire, East Anglia, Sussex, Kent and the Isle of Wight, sizeable plantings have been made, English viticulture is being reborn, and English wine is now available, though not in large quantities as yet by commercial standards. But by 1980 enough groundwork had been done and experience gained to show that grape growing in southern England *could* be a viable proposition, and the English Vineyards Association was flourishing. As those vineyards expand the number of hectares under cultivation by continual propagation there is every hope now that a sizeable English viticulture will emerge.

The truth is that the growing and the training of vines is so straightforward that *all* who are interested in winemaking should try it; vines occupy little space, they can be planted at the back of flower borders, along fences, beside paths, or on a south-facing wall. They make ideal screens, and they interfere little with flower or salad crops, for they are deep- and not surface-rooting. They are as easy to grow as, say, raspberries and blackcurrants. If they are grown espalier fashion along a wire fence it is the work of a moment to throw mats or polythene sheeting over them to protect them from frost, or netting to prevent depredations by birds when the grapes ripen.

The all-important point is to make sure, when you choose your vines, that you select only the earliest cropping varieties.

Just as the Englishman classes his potatoes, as 'first earlies', 'second earlies', 'maincrop', and so on, according to when the crop is ready, so the Frenchman talks of his vines as 'première epoque', 'deuxième epoque' or 'troisième epoque' (first, second, or third epoch). Thus early ripeners are all of the '1ère époque', and very early ones the '1ère époque prècoce'. These will all ripen well in our English climate, whereas 2nd or 3rd epoch vines will not. Black Hamburg, for instance, which is perhaps the most generally known grape in this country, is only so because it was once widely cultivated in greenhouses, but it is unsuitable for outdoor use here, being of the second epoch.

Vineyards in the south of England are roughly the same latitude (49–50°) as Germany, where it is found that white grapes will ripen satisfactorily, but not red. Not surprisingly that has now been proved to be generally the case in England. So plump for an early-ripening, white, outdoor wine grape such as grown in Germany.

Those recommended grape varieties for commercial growing for good quality wine, which is a good guide for amateurs, are: Huxelrebe, Madeline Angevine, Muller Thurgau, Reichensteiner, Schonburger, and Seyval Blanc.

Also authorised for growing in the UK are: Auxerrois, Bacchus, Chardonnay, Ehrenfelser, Faber, Kerner, Madeline Sylvaner, Ortega, Pinot Noir (Red), Rulander, Siegerrebe, Baco No 1 (Red), and Wrotham Pinot (Red).

Consult your nurseryman, or better still a specialist vinegrower such as Cranmore Vineyard, Yarmouth, Isle of Wight; Jackman's Nurseries of Woking; W. L. Cardy, Lower Bowden, Pangbourne, Berks; S. Skelton, Smeeth, Ashford, Kent; D. Pritchard, Wooton Courtenay, Minehead, Somerset; Greenland Nurseries, Clayton West, Huddersfield; and J. R. M. Donald, West Tytherley, nr Salisbury, Wilts. Many nurserymen can supply the more popular varieties.

It is not the intention to discuss viticulture in detail here, for many excellent technical books are available on the subject, but only to give, as it were, a few pointers to the complete novice.

Firstly, if you are planting many vines, do not have all the same variety. Obtaining satisfaction from your vines will be a long-term project and it is best to choose several different vines and grow them experimentally rather than make a large outlay on one variety which may prove disappointing. Nor need this be expensive, for cuttings from friends' vines can easily be rooted. Then select the ones that do best in your soil. Secondly, remember that vines fall into two main categories, producing wine grapes or dessert grapes, and that in each case black and white grapes of varying sweetness are obtainable.

So decide what type of grape you want, and choose some early burgeoning varieties to meet your need.

Although because of Phylloxera vine weevils, commercial vinegrowers are bound to use vines grafted on American rootstocks, which are resistant to Phylloxera, this does not necessarily apply to amateur growers. Vines are easily propagated by simply taking and rooting ripe cuttings in the autumn. But it is much safer, and definitely better for viticulture as a whole, to buy vines grafted on to American rootstocks. This way your vines will be less susceptible to disease, and less likely to pass any infections on to any commercial vineyards in your area. And remember that commercial vineyards stretch at least as far north as the Midlands! And the winged adult Phylloxera insects can fly, and travel many miles on a suitable breeze. The American rootstock resists the vine louse or phylloxera which is the scourge of the *Vitis vinifera*, or Continental varieties. The phylloxera kills off the vinifera by destroying the root system, but the American *Vinis rupestris* stands up to it satisfactorily.

It is as well, too, to give your vine grower as much accurate information as you can about your soil, so that he can the better advise you.

You can either grow vines from cuttings or purchase them when 1–2 years old, and plant them in spring or autumn.

Planting

If you have them in a row or rows in the garden, growing on a waist high fence (which is a practical system because they are then much more controllable and more easily protected), they should be at least a metre apart, preferably more, and there should be a metre between rows.

When the vine arrives, if it has not been pruned, cut it down to the lowest two buds on each branch; even if it is 3 metres high this *must* be done, or it will never grow grapes of any consequence.

The reason for this drastic pruning, and for those of subsequent years, is that for three years at least you should concentrate upon building up a really strong and extensive root system, and not top growth, otherwise the vine can never be really strong and prolific. Therefore the growth above ground must be curtailed so that all the strength of the plant will go into developing its roots until in the fourth year it is allowed to fruit. So vinegrowing, as you can see, is rather a long-term affair. Luckily winemakers are used to exercising patience!

Choose a sunny position for your vine, facing south if possible, dig a hole big enough to allow the roots ample room, and place the vine in position. Space out the roots well, and cover with light soil mixed with silver sand and old compost until the hole is filled. Be sure to tread well in.

As with raspberries, the fruit of the vine is borne on the wood of the previous year, so if a vine is spring planted you *could* obtain your first grapes in 18 months (though they will be scanty and it is better not to let the vine fruit). Certainly no more than two or three bunches should be allowed to form, or the strength of the vine will be sapped, but from then on a few more may be allowed each year until, in about four years, the vine will be cropping well.

As the fruit begins to ripen keep a close eye on it, and cover it either with netting or with high cloches or the birds will have it first. When the grapes are thoroughly ripe they are pressed, yeast is added, and they are fermented in the usual way (see under 'Grape Wine').

From cuttings

If growing from cuttings, take your cuttings in the autumn. You need

The author shows Evelyn Barrett, editor of Homebrew Today, *his small vineyard. Here there are Baco. No. 1 (black) and Seyval (white) vines. On the house wall there are Seyval vines and on the kitchen garden wall, Merlot.*

Seyval grapes in August, about two-thirds grown. They ripen in late October.

pieces of stem about 9 in (25 cm) long, with a pair of buds at either end. Bury these 30 cm or so deep, laying them horizontally, so that they will survive the winter, and in late March or early April dig them up, and set them just like any other cutting, with the topmost two buds at ground level. Sift some light soil in a little mound over the cutting (about 1½ in. high will do) to prevent the wind from drying it out, or frost damage, mark the spot with a cane, and await results.

There are many ways of pruning, and training vines, and I have favoured the idea of growing them on the wall of the house and on wires in a garden cage, both of which have been successful over the years. Birds are the main menace, blackbirds in particular going crazy to get at the wall grapes as they ripen. We have to net those too.

An important point to note is that you *must* leave the grapes on the vine as long as possible in order that they may fully ripen. In our part of the south of England, for instance, I find that white grape varieties such as Muller Thurgau or Seyval are never really ready for picking before about October 20, and possibly later. Harvesting of red grapes, which take longer to ripen, often has to be delayed even into November, and on several occasions I have had to pick them with a heavy frost upon them. Grapes can be left quite safely to gain the maximum ripeness as long as a close watch is kept for any sign of mildew, when they should be harvested rapidly and any affected berries cut away.

See October recipes for method of vintning.

Wines by purpose

Modern winemakers tend to make wines for a purpose rather than by ingredient, and to blend two or more fruits or ingredients to produce the particular type of wine they want (e.g. white, table, dry) rather than one named after a single ingredient. In other words, what ingredient is used is to them unimportant; what matters is the final wine.

Six main types are commonly recognised – aperitif, table, dessert, social, rosé and sparkling – and they are defined thus:

Aperitif A wine that stimulates one's appetite. Can be dry or sweet. Bitter flavours popular. Anything from 5–14 per cent alcohol.

Table wine For drinking with a meal. Dry or slightly sweet. Not too strong in bouquet. About 10 per cent to 12 per cent alcohol.

Social wine For drinking while watching the telly! The most popular of all – a wine for social purposes, other than with food. In between a table wine and a dessert wine for flavour and sweetness. Around 14 per cent alcohol. Many of the wines in this book are of this type.

Rosé   Pink (not 'from roses', necessarily). Delicate, fresh, medium dry or sweet. An excellent compromise wine for table use.

Dessert wine   Rich in body, bouquet, flavour and alcohol, so that it can be served at the end of a meal. It can be medium to sweet, and can be white, golden, red or tawny. Commercial dessert wines (e.g. port) may be fortified. Amateur dessert wines are usually not, and certainly not in most competitions.

Sparkling wine   That most delightful of wines. Usually about 10 per cent alcohol but with an intoxicating power greater than one would expect because the carbon dioxide carries the effect to the head more quickly!

The essential thing is to realise that what we try to do is to produce a 'balanced' wine; strength of flavour, acidity, sweetness, and percentage alcohol should all increase proportionately from a light dry wine at one end of the scale to a heavy, sweet, dessert wine at the other. While all these components should be distinguishable not one of them should be too obtrusive.

Thus in light dry wines we shall probably use 2½ – 3 lb (1.1 – 1.3 kilos) of fruit per gallon (4.5 litres), in medium social wines 5 – 6 lb (2 – 2.5 kilos) and in dessert wines upwards of 6 lb (2.5 kilos).

Sugar similarly: light dry wines 2¼ lb (1 kilo), medium 2½ – 3 lb (1.1 – 1.3 kilo) and dessert 3½ lb (1.5 kilos).

And acid: light dry 2 teaspoons (10 ml), medium 3 teaspoons (15 ml) and dessert 4 teaspoons (20 ml).

To illustrate this in practical fashion here are a few of my favourite recipes of each type.

*   Aperitif (dry)

Ingredients	Metric	British	USA
Seville oranges	6	6	5
Sweet oranges	6	6	5
Sugar	1 kilo	2¼ lb	1¾ lb
Water to	4.5 litres	1 gallon	1 gallon
Sherry yeast and nutrient			

Wash the oranges in warm water to remove any wax and peel three of each, keeping the peel thin and avoiding the pith, which imparts a very bitter flavour. Boil 3 litres (5¼ pints) of water and then add the peel to it; cover, and allow to stand for 24 hours to extract the zest. Then strain the infusion into a polythene bucket containing the sugar, and the juice of all twelve oranges. Stir until all the sugar is dissolved, and then add the yeast and yeast nutrient. Cover the bucket closely and stand in a warm place (20°C) for four or five days, after which the ferment will have quietened a little and the liquor can be poured into a fermenting jar, made up to 4.5 litres, and a trap fitted. Leave until it clears, then rack and bottle as usual.

*   Table white (dry)

Ingredients	Metric	British	USA
Fresh apricots	1.3 kilo	3 lb	2¼ lb
White grape concentrate	200 ml	¼ pint	¼ pint
or Sultanas (white raisins)	450 g	1 lb	¾ lb
White sugar	900 g	2 lb	1½ lb
Pectic enzyme	5 g	1 teaspoon	1 teaspoon
Water to	4.5 litres	1 gallon	1 gallon
GP wine yeast and nutrient			

Wash and 'stone' the apricots, then chop them up with the sultanas and place in a bucket. Cover them with almost 4.5 litres (1 gallon) of cold water, add a Campden tablet and the pectic enzyme. Cover and leave for a week, stirring daily. Strain and press out the fruit, stir in the sugar, activated yeast and nutrient, place in a 4.5 litre (1 gallon) jar and ferment out under an airlock. This can be drunk at Christmas, but is better for keeping 6–9 months.

* Table white (dry)

Ingredients	Metric	British	USA
Windfall apples	5 kilos	11 lb	9 lb
White sugar to gallon of must	1 kilo	2¼ lb	1½ lb
White grape concentrate	200 ml	¼ pint	¼ pint
Pectic enzyme	5 g	1 teaspoon	1 teaspoon
Campden tablet	1	1	1
GP wine yeast and nutrient			

The above to each 4.5 litres (1 gallon) of must

Use mixed apples and, if possible, let a tenth of them be crab or cooking apples. Cut out damaged or maggoty portions and chop or smash the apples. Put the pulp in a bin and add just enough water to cover them. Add Campden tablet and pectic enzyme and allow to stand, covered, for 24 hours; then stir in the yeast and nutrient.

Ferment the pulp for about a week, rousing it from the bottom each day and keeping all the pulp wet: it often smells horrible, but do not worry!

Strain and press the pulp and stir in 1 kg of sugar and 200 ml grape concentrate to each 4.5 litres, or 1 gallon jar full. Put the liquid in jars under airlocks and ferment out in the usual way. Rack when clear and add 1 Campden tablet to each 4.5 litres.

* Table red (dry)

Ingredients	Metric	British	USA
Blackberries	1.3 kilos	3 lb	2¼ lb
Sloes	450 g	1 lb	¾ lb
Sugar	1.1 kilos	2½ lb	2 lb
Malic acid	2 g	½ teaspoon	½ teaspoon
Tannin	2 g	½ teaspoon	½ teaspoon
Pectic enzyme	5 g	1 teaspoon	1 teaspoon
Water	4.5 litres	1 gallon	1 gallon
GP wine yeast and nutrient			

Mash the sloes and blackberries in 4.5 litres (8 pints) of boiling water, add sugar, nutrient and acid. When cooled to 20°C add tannin and pectic enzyme.

Add active yeast after 24 hours. Ferment on pulp for four days, then strain off into a demijohn, and ferment to dryness.

* Social wine golden

Ingredients	Metric	British	USA
Peaches	2.5 kilos	5 lb	4 lb
Bananas (ripe)	2	2	2
White grape concentrate	250 g	½ lb	½ lb
Sugar	900 g	2 lb	1½ lb
Citric acid	10 g	2 teaspoons	2 teaspoons
Tannin	2 g	½ teaspoon	½ teaspoon
Pectic enzyme	5 g	1 teaspoon	1 teaspoon
Campden tablets	3	3	3
Water	4 litres	7 pints	6 pints
GP wine yeast and nutrient			

Halve the peaches, and discard the stones and skins; chop, crush or liquidise the fruit and add to the water.

Peel, crush or liquidise the bananas, add the grape juice, the citric acid, pectic enzyme and one crushed Campden tablet. Add all to the peaches and water, cover and leave for 24 hours.

Add an activated yeast, nutrient and tannin, loosely cover the bin and ferment on the pulp for three days, keeping the pulp submerged.

Strain the pulp out into a nylon bag or sieve, rolling to help extract juice, but do not press it. Stir the sugar into the juice, pour into a fermentation jar, fit an airlock and ferment down to specific gravity of 1.000.

Rack the wine into a clean demijohn containing 1 g (¼ teaspoon) of potassium sorbate and one crushed Campden tablet, to terminate fermentation. Add some wine finings, leave the wine in a cool place, and as soon as it is bright and clear rack again.

111

When fermentation is finished rack into sterilised storage jars, add 1 Campden tablet per gallon and keep for two months. Rack again and if necessary add wine finings.

As soon as the wine is bright, rack again and store until it is six months old, then bottle.

* Social wine red

Ingredients	Metric	British	USA
Damsons	1.5 kilos	4 lb	3 lb
Sugar	1.3 kilos	3 lb	2 ¼ lb
Red grape concentrate	150 ml	¼ pint	¼ pint
Water	4.5 litres	1 gallon	1 gallon
Pectic enzyme	5 g	1 teaspoon	1 teaspoon
GP wine yeast and nutrient			

Put the water on to boil, then crush the damsons in a bowl or crock with half the sugar. Pour the boiling water over them, stir really well to dissolve the sugar, and allow to cool to about 24°C before adding the pectic enzyme and covering closely. A day later add the yeast and yeast nutrient. Cover again and leave for 48 hours in a warm place to allow a good fermentation to start. Put the remaining sugar in a polythene bucket or other vessel and strain the liquor on to it. In this case a nylon sieve or muslin is often not fine enough, and it pays to use a jelly bag to be sure of the wine clearing.

Do not squeeze the bag to express the last of the juice, or you will cloud the wine; give it time to run through naturally. It pays to be patient here. Stir well to ensure that all sugar is thoroughly dissolved, then pour into fermenting vessel and fit an airlock to allow ferment to finish. (It might be slow to start again after you have used the jelly bag, but do not worry about this; enough yeast will pass through to cause a ferment, but you must give it time to multiply again.) Rack when the wine is really clear, and again three months later if a second yeast deposit is thrown, then bottle in dark bottles. If the wine is too dry for your liking add a touch of sugar but in that case add more sulphite or other stabiliser as well.

* Rosé medium

Use *red* rosepetals, fresh and undamaged, to make this light, well scented wine.

Ingredients	Metric	British	USA
Fragrant rose petals	2.25 litres	4 pints	4 pints
Sugar	1 kilo	2¼ lb	1½ lb
White grape concentrate	300 ml	½ pint	½ pint
Citric acid	5 g	1 teaspoon	1 teaspoon
Tartaric acid	5 g	1 teaspoon	1 teaspoon
Grape tannin	3 g	1 teaspoon	1 teaspoon
Pectic enzyme	5 g	1 teaspoon	1 teaspoon
Water to	4.5 litres	1 gallon	1 gallon
Hock yeast and nutrient			

Put the rose petals in a plastic bucket with the sugar, grape concentrate and additives above. Pour on 3.3 litres (6 pints) of cold water. Stir, add one Campden tablet and cover. Leave for 24 hours before adding active yeast starter, and ferment on the flowers for four days at 20°C. Strain liquid into one-gallon jar and ferment on under an airlock until SG falls below 1.000. Rack, top up and add one Campden tablet. This wine is drinkable within a few weeks, but improves, greatly for up to two years. Sweeten to taste before drinking.

* Rosé (dry)

Ingredients	Metric	British	USA
Ripe Victoria plums	2.7 kilos	6 lb	5 lb
Sugar	1 kilo	2¼ lb	1½ lb
Port type grape concentrate	150 ml	¼ pint	¼ pint
Pectic enzyme	5 g	1 teaspoon	1 teaspoon
Citric acid	5 g	1 teaspoon	1 teaspoon
Tannin	2.5 g	½ teaspoon	½ teaspoon
Water	4.5 litres	1 gallon	1 gallon
Bordeaux yeast and nutrient			

Cut the plums in half, crush well with your hands. Boil ½ gallon water   113 and pour over the pulp. Leave for five hours, then add the rest of the water, cold, and the enzyme, tannin and citric acid. Leave for two days and strain. You should have a gallon of clear juice. Bring this just to the boil, and pour it over the sugar, stirring to dissolve. Allow the liquor to cool to 21°C then add the yeast. Pour the whole into your fermentation jar and fit an airlock. When the wine begins to clear, siphon it off for the first time, and when all the fermentation has stopped rack again into clean bottles and cork; mature for at least a year.

* Hoddesdon white dessert (by John Grindell)

Ingredients	Metric	British	USA
Gooseberries, crushed (do not break pips)	1.8 kilo	4 lb	3 lb
Bananas, peeled and sliced	900 g	2 lb	1½ lb
White grape concentrate	570 ml	1 pint	1 pint
Apple juice	1.15 litres	2 pints	1¾ pints
Sultanas (white raisins)	225 g	½ lb	½ lb
Tartaric or citric acid	3 g	½ teaspoon	½ teaspoon
Yeast nutrient	5 g	1 teaspoon	1 teaspoon
Vitamin B₁ tablet	1	1	1
Sugar (in syrup form)	900 g	2 lb	1½ lb
Water to	4.5 litres	1 gallon	1 gallon
Pectin destroying enzyme	5 g	1 teaspoon	1 teaspoon
GP wine yeast			

Put the ingredients into a bucket; for a wine with a better bouquet, add a quart of rose petals or one head of elderflowers. Add 2 crushed Campden tablets per gallon. Leave 24 hours, then add active wine yeast. Stir twice daily for at least 5 days. Strain liquid from solids. Put fermenting liquid into gallon jar with an airlock.

If SG has dropped substantially at this stage a further 225 g (½ lb) sugar in syrup form may be added. If SG has not dropped a lot, leave a further week or so before adding extra sugar.

Hoddesdon red dessert (by John Grindell)

Ingredients	Metric	British	USA
Black cherries (squashed to split skins)	1.8 kilos	4 lb	3 lb
Bananas, peeled and sliced	900 g	2 lb	1½ lb
Red grape concentrate	570 ml	1 quart	1½ pints
Orange juice (unsweetened)	1.15 litre	1 quart	1½ pints
Sultanas (white raisins)	225 g	½ lb	½ lb
Dried elderberries	225 g	½ lb	½ lb
Yeast nutrient	5 g	1 teaspoon	1 teaspoon
Vitamin B_1 tablet	1	1	1
Sugar, in syrup form	900 g	2 lb	1½ lb
Tartaric or citric acid	3 g	½ teaspoon	½ teaspoon
Add 2 crushed Campden tablets per gallon			
Bordeaux or Burgundy wine yeast			
Water to	4.5 litres	1 gallon	1 gallon

Put 6 pints water and all the ingredients except the yeast into a bucket. Leave for 24 hours. Add active wine yeast. Stir twice daily for at least 5 days. Strain and put fermenting liquid into 4.5 litres (1 gallon) jar.

Subsequently, add a further 225 g (½ lb) sugar in syrup form, and further 110 g (4 oz) lots of sugar syrup as long as the wine will take it and keep fermenting, topping up finally to 1 gallon.

Rack off any heavy sediment as and when required.

Sparkling gooseberry

Ingredients	Metric	British	USA
Hard but ripe green gooseberries	1.5 kilos	3¼ lb	2¼ lb
Hock style concentrated grape juice	250 g	9 oz	7 oz
Sugar	675 g	1½ lb	1 lb
Citric acid	5 g	1 teaspoon	1 teaspoon
Pectic enzyme	5 g	1 teaspoon	1 teaspoon
Campden tablets	2	2	2
Water to	4.5 litres	1 gallon	1 gallon

Wash, top and tail the gooseberries. Pour 6 pints of boiling water over them and when cool squash the berries by hand. Add acid, pectic enzyme and one Campden tablet, cover and leave for 24 hours. Stir in grape juice, yeast and nutrient, and ferment on the pulp for four days, pressing down the fruit cap twice daily. Strain and press the fruit. Stir in the sugar to dissolve and pour must into fermentation jar. Top up to 1 gallon and ferment on under an airlock until dry.

Rack into clean jar, adding Campden tablet, and when wine is bright, rack again. Now inoculate wine with 70 g (2½ oz) caster sugar and active champagne yeast starter. Fit an airlock, and as soon as the wine starts fermenting again pour it into six heavy champagne bottles. Fit hollow-domed plastic stoppers or Sparkletops, wire them down and store for two weeks at room temperature and then in the cool.

*   Sparkling pomagne

Ingredients	Metric	British	USA
Bramley cooking apples	2 kilos	4½ lb	3½ lb
Hard Conference pears	1 kilo	2¼ lb	2 lb
Chaenomeles japonica quince	250 g	9 oz	7 oz
White grape juice concentrate	250 g	9 oz	7 oz
Sugar	675 g	1½ lb	1 lb
Pectic enzyme	5 g	1 teaspoon	1 teaspoon
Campden tablets	3	3	3
Water	3.5 litres	6 pints	5 pints
Champagne yeast and nutrient			

Wash and mash the fruit and drop it into a bin containing the pectic enzyme and one Campden tablet dissolved in the water. Cover and leave for 24 hours.

Stir in the grape juice, one-third of the sugar, the yeast and nutrient and ferment on the pulp for seven days, always keeping the must submerged.

Strain out and press the fruit, stir in the rest of the sugar, pour the must into a fermentation jar, fit an airlock and ferment to dryness.

Rack into a clean jar, add one crushed Campden tablet and when the wine is bright, rack it again and store for six months.

Stir in 70 g (2½ oz) caster sugar and an active champagne yeast, fit an airlock and stand the jar in a warm place for a few hours.

Sterilise the champagne bottles and hollow-domed plastic stoppers with suitable cages.

As soon as the wine is fermenting, pour it into the bottles, fit the stoppers and wire down the cages.

Leave the bottles in a warm room for one week then store in the cool for a further six months.

Country wines

One of the exciting things about making country wines is the wide range of ingredients you have at your disposal to make wines of a vast variety of flavours. Better still, many of these ingredients are free!

There are five main sources: fruit, flowers, vegetables, grain, and leaf or shoot (which includes herbs).

Obviously, it is a delight to use surplus crops from your garden, and you have the advantage of knowing that your own fruit, vegetables and flowers are safe, because you know whether they have been sprayed or not.

If, on the other hand, you are gathering, say, dandelions or elderberries, avoid doing so alongside a heavily-trafficked main road, where they will have been contaminated with lead from exhaust fumes, or from the edge of a crop field which may have been sprayed with chemicals.

Some plants and flowers are so poisonous that they must on no account be used for winemaking. Others are 'doubtful' in that they may not be highly poisonous, particularly in the small quantities in which they might be employed in winemaking, but must still be highly suspect. The position is complicated by the fact that some substances used in winemaking, notably sugar and yeast, can sometimes neutralise poisons, so that occasionally safe wines may be made from apparently doubtful sources. But one cannot depend on this and we would urge winemakers **NOT** to use anything in the 'poisonous' or 'doubtful' categories. Our lists are by no means exhaustive and the only safe rule is: if in doubt about a material – don't use it.

Poisonous

Acacia, aconite, alder, aquilegia, azalea, baneberry, belladonna, berberis, black nightshade, bluebell, buckthorn, dried broom, buttercup, celandine, columbine, charlock, Christmas rose, clematis, cotoneaster, cowbane, crocus, cuckoopint, cyclamen, daffodil, dahlia, deadly nightshade, delphinium, dwarf elder, fool's parsley, foxglove, most fungi, geranium, green potatoes, all hellebores, hemlock, henbane, holly, honeysuckle (the berries), horse-chestnut, laburnum, laurel, lilac, lily-of-the-valley, lobelia, lupin, marsh marigolds, meadow rue, mezereon, mistletoe, monkshood, narcissus, orchid, pheasant's eye, pæony, poppy, privet, rhododendron, rhubarb leaves, spearwort, spindleberry, sweet pea, thorn apple, tomato stems or foliage, traveller's joy, wood anemone, woody nightshade, yew.

Doubtful

Borage, broom, carnation, chrysanthemum, clover, pinks.

Whether the material comes from your garden or from the hedgerow, see that it is sound, to avoid mouldy flavours, and in any case wash and sulphite it well. If boiling water is used in the recipe it will kill most bacteria, but if you use a cold water recipe it is essential to do the same by using sulphite 24 hours before introducing your yeast.

Ingredients are also to be found on the shelves of your home brew shop or supermarket: grape concentrate, tinned and boiled fruit, dried fruit, concentrated juices, pulps and purées and grains.

Fruit wines

Popular fruits are:

Apple   Eating, cider or crab. A versatile ingredient for all types of white wine. Blends well. Good for making 'sherries' because it oxidises easily. High in pectin.

Apricot   Almost as good as the peach; a delicate flavour. High in pectin.

Banana   A good wine for blending. For improved body use 1–2 lb in a gallon of wine made from another main ingredient. Can be used as clearing agent.

Bilberry   Best of all the reds. Same family as blueberry. Main food of grouse! Hard to pick but a glorious flavour. Can be bought bottled (Krakus). Not now available dried.

Cherry   Morello best.

Currants   Both black and red good, but high in pectin and acid.

Elderberry Several kinds (blue and white). Choose best. Slightly coarse flavour, but excellent when blended with, say, banana, damson, sloe, apple or grape concentrate.

Fig Makes an excellent wine with not too pronounced a flavour.

Gooseberry 'The hairy grape'. Excellent winemaking material, especially for sparkling wines.

Grape Own growing or bought. Dried grapes (sultanas, raisins, currants). Grape concentrate.

Hawthornberry Produces a rather bitter wine of no great distinction.

Mulberry Hard to come by, but makes an excellent port-type wine for long maturing.

Orange Good for aperitif wines.

Peach The best of all, particularly for social and dessert wines. Imported peaches are cheapest in August. Dried or tinned types can be employed. High in pectin.

Plum Lots of pectin. Use only a short pulp fermentation, five days or less.

Prune Makes a good dry wine, with a pleasant flavour.

Raisin, Sultana (See grape).

Raspberry Deep red; heavy bouquet; good for improving bouquet of other red wines, but too strong on its own.

Rhubarb (fruit or vegetable?) Treated as fruit because it is made like a fruit wine. Allow for high acidity. Leaves poisonous.

Rowanberry Rather too bitter a flavour used alone for wine but can be useful in aperitifs.

Sloe Light red. A short pulp fermentation is advised or kernels will flavour wine.

Strawberry Best for rosé or light red wines. Flavour fresh and delicate.

Dried fruit

Available are:

Apricots, apples, bananas, elderberries, peaches, raisins, sultanas, currants and figs.

Generally speaking, dried fruits can be substituted for fresh fruit at the rate of 1 – 4. (Dried fruit weighs a quarter as much as fresh fruit owing to the weight of water removed.) So for 1 lb fresh fruit substitute 4 oz dried.

The best method to use is the 'pouring on boiling water and soaking' one, after thorough rinsing in warm water.

Tinned fruit

Canned or bottled fruit can also be used, and is usually employed at 2 – 3 lb (1 – 1.5 kilo) per gallon (4.5 litres).

Pour any syrup from tins into fermenting jar. Mash the fruit with a stainless steel spoon and put into polythene bucket. Boil 4 pints water and dissolve 2¼ lb sugar in it and pour this boiling syrup over the fruit. Allow to cool to 21 °C before adding acid, tannin and depectiniser. Stir well, cover and leave in a warm place. Next day stir, pour the whole into the fermenting jar with the syrup from the cans, and add yeast, nutrient and enough cold water to bring level of must to just below shoulder of jar, leaving room for a 'head'. Fit an airlock, leave in a warm place for 10 days, shaking daily to disperse pulp through liquid. Then strain into a fresh jar, top up with water, fit an airlock, and ferment out.

Flower wines

Do *not* use protected wild flowers. Some possible flowers are:

Broom (March to May). Use only fresh flowers: cases of illness have occurred after drinking wine made with dried broom flowers.

Burnet (Greater Salad Burnet, *Sanguisorba officinalis*). (June/September). Sturdy red colour and rich flavour.

Coltsfoot (February/May).

Dandelion (St George's Day, 23rd April!).

Elderflower (Choose sweet-scented and not rank variety).

Golden rod (From the garden).

Gorse (Long blooming season).

120   **Hawthorn** (May/June).

Honeysuckle (June/July wild or cultivated). Flowers only: berries and foliage are poisonous.

Pansy (From the garden).

Primrose (Lovely scent).

Roses (Garden roses, old-fashioned damask roses are the best, with heavy scent).

Flower wines are made by the soaking method, either hot or cold, a brief soaking (up to 2 days) with hot water, and up to a week with cold.

Usually a quart to a gallon of flower heads to the gallon of water is required.

Dried flowers can also be used.

Dried dandelions	1 oz =	4 pints fresh =	2¼ litres
Dried rosepetals	1 oz =	5 pints fresh =	2¾ litres
Dried elderflowers	1 oz =	8 pints fresh =	4½ litres
Dried coltsfoot	1 oz =	4 pints fresh =	2¼ litres
Dried parsley	1 oz =	½ lb fresh =	227 g
Dried rosehip shells	1 oz =	4 pints fresh =	2¼ litres

Vegetable wines

Beetroot Good deep colour at first but this is usually unstable. Best in a blended wine, otherwise a slight earthy flavour.

Carrot Good in blended wines (with grain) but colour often unstable.

Mangold Makes a good dry wine but I find it a 'moving' experience.

Peapod wine Far better than it sounds!

Parsnip An excellent wine, in Hampshire known as 'tanglefoot' for fairly obvious reasons. Parsnips are high in sugar and pectin.

Potato Often used in recipes but contribute little to a wine except starch and therefore a possible haze.

Rhubarb Excellent material but fairly acid: make allowances for that.

Sugarbeet 4–6 roots make an excellent gallon of dry white wine.

Amounts recommended vary, but usually 4–6 lb per gallon. All these vegetables require the boiling method. The root is scrubbed and cut into half-inch slices and then boiled in some or all of the water.

Grain wines

Wheat Usually used with raisins or grape concentrate to produce a brown wine with a good 'bite'.

Barley A similar but slightly heavier and smoother wine.

Rye Rarely used for winemaking though it is sometimes used by beer brewers.

Rice Used with raisins makes a really excellent 'quickie' wine with a real kick.

Used in most recipes at the rate of 1 lb per gallon. Grains need soaking overnight in a pint or two of water to soften them so that they can be put through a mincer easily before being incorporated in the must.

Best method to employ is the 'pour on boiling water' one, and it is important to include raisins, sultanas or grape concentrate to impart a vinous character to the finished wine.

Leaf shoot or herb wines

Balm For a scented wine.

Bramble tips A pleasant rosé wine.

Mint Excellent in cold cups.

Nettletops Not a favourite of mine.

Oak leaves Young or old can be used.

Parsley Makes an excellent dry white wine; 1 lb to gallon.

Vine leaf wine Truly good white, often better than that from the grape of the same vine.

Most of these wines are made by the 'pour on boiling water' method, and all are improved by the inclusion of 150 ml grape concentrate per gallon.

Recipes the year round

The recipes in this book are given under the months in which they are usually made, so that your winemaking can be practised all the year round, but they are also indexed alphabetically at the back of the book so that any one can be quickly found.

As I have said, there are two schools of thought about recipes. Some prefer always to use a gallon (4.5 litres) of water, and use the resultant surplus for topping up; others prefer to do calculations so that they arrive at a final quantity of exactly one gallon.

We find the second method complicates things for the winemaker rather too much. When all is said and done, recipes are at best a general guide to quantities of ingredients, and slight variations (except in the case of sugar and acid) make but little difference.

For this reason we have stuck to using 1 gallon of liquid in most cases but if you wish to use to make precisely one gallon, and not more, it is quite simple. In that case never start with more than six pints of water and reduce the sugar quantities shown by 5 oz (140 g) for a dry wine, 8 oz (225 g) for a medium and 10 oz (280 g) for a sweet. Make the wine otherwise as suggested, topping up to 1 gallon finally.

Since Britain has now gone metric but there are many who still prefer to work in imperial measures we still give both, with USA quantities as well. It should be noted that weights do not always correspond exactly because, as I say, a recipe is only a guide and figures have been rounded up and down to give a 'tidy' and logical figure in each scale. Exact metric equivalents are given in Appendix A on pages 227/8, but here are some measures which it is useful to have to hand:

Liquid

British pints	Cups, glasses, etc	Fluid oz
⅛ pint	1 sherry glass (½ gill)	2½ fl oz
⅛ pint +	1 wine glass (¾ gill)	3 fl oz
¼ pint (American)	—	4 fl oz
¼ pint	1 gill	5 fl oz
⅓ pint	1 teacup (approx.)	6⅔ fl oz
½ pint	1 British (breakfast) cup	10 fl oz
½ pint (American)	1 American cup	8 fl oz
⁴/₅ pint	1 American pint	16 fl oz
1 pint	2 British Standard cups	20 fl oz
1¾ pints	1 litre	35 fl oz
2 pints	1 quart	40 fl oz
8 pints (American)	1 gallon (American)	128 fl oz
8 pints	1 gallon	160 fl oz

American measures

American readers should note that the pound measure of weight as now used is the same in Britain, Canada, and USA (it equals roughly ½ kilo) but the British and American gallons differ.

The imperial or English gallon as used in Britain and Canada is of 8 pints, 160 liquid ounces, or 277¼ cubic inches, whereas the USA gallon is of 8 pints, 128 liquid ounces, or 231 cubic inches. (The American fluid ounce is slightly larger than the British, 16 USA ounces equalling 16½ British ounces.) The English gallon thus equals 1.2 USA gallons. This accounts for the fact that in the recipes smaller quantities of ingredients are specified for use with the smaller USA gallon.

A quick comparison therefore is:

British	1	2	3	4	5	gallons
American	1¼	2½	3½	4¾	6	gallons

There are differences in spoon measures, too. The American teaspoon is only four-fifths the size of the British, but this difference can usually be ignored, since it is cancelled out by the fact that the gallon is also smaller. Two British teaspoons equal one dessertspoon, and two dessertspoons one tablespoon, but the American 'tablespoon' is the same size as the British 'dessertspoon'. This is allowed for in the recipes; all measures are in *level* and not 'rounded' or heaped spoonsful, *using a standard measuring teaspoon (5 ml)*.

Spoons, British	Spoons, American	Fluid oz
—	1 teaspoon	⅛ fl oz
1 teaspoon	—	⅛ fl oz
1 dessertspoon	1 tablespoon	¼ fl oz
1 tablespoon	1 serving spoon	½ fl oz

In all the recipes use, preferably, a wine yeast, but failing that a level teaspoon of granulated yeast per gallon.

It is good practice to add 1 Campden tablet to each gallon of must 24 hours before adding the yeast, and always to use a yeast nutrient.

If you are diabetic and wish to make a safe wine always use the minimum sugar (2–2½ lb to the gallon, 250 g per litre) and a nutrient to ensure that you ferment it right out to dryness. The wine can be sweetened to taste when finished with Sorbitol if desired.

124

* Barley wine (medium)

Ingredients	Metric	British	USA
Barley	½ kilo	1 lb	¾ lb
Grape concentrate	280 ml	½ pint	½ pint
Lemons	2	2	2
Sugar	1.3 kilos	3 lb	2½ lb
Amylozyme	As directed		
Campden tablet	1	1	1
Yeast and nutrient			
Water	4.5 litres	1 gallon	1 gallon

A pound of raisins can be substituted for the grape concentrate and 4 level teaspoons of citric acid for the lemons if desired.

Grind the barley and raisins in a mincer, having soaked the grain in a pint of water overnight. Put sugar, barley and raisins in a polythene bucket and pour on hot (not necessarily boiling) water.

Add the juice of the lemons or the citric acid. Allow to cool until tepid, then add the Amylozyme and the crushed Campden tablet. Cover and leave for 24 hours, then introduce the yeast and nutrient. Cover closely and leave for 8 days, stirring daily, then strain into fermenting vessel, top up to bottom of neck with cold water, and fit an airlock. Siphon off into bottles when clear, adding 1 crushed Campden tablet beforehand. Ready in about six months.

* Fig wine (medium)

	Ingredients	Metric	British	USA
	Brown sugar	1 kilo	2½ lb	2 lb
	Dried figs	1 kilo	2 lb	1½ lb
	Large raisins	¼ kilo	½ lb	½ lb
or	Concentrate (white)	140 ml	¼ pint	¼ pint
	Lemon	1	1	1
	Orange	1	1	1
	Boiling water	4.5 litres	1 gallon	1 gallon
	Yeast and nutrient			

125

January

Chop the figs and raisins and place in a polythene bucket with the sugar, the grated lemon and orange rinds (no white pith) and the juice of the two fruits; a cupful of grape concentrate can be used instead of the raisins. Bring the water to the boil, and pour it over the ingredients, stirring well to dissolve the sugar, and adding one crushed Campden tablet. When the liquor has cooled to about 20°C, cool enough for you to be able to put your finger in it comfortably, stir in the yeast, cover the bucket closely, and leave it in a warm place (about 21°C) for 12 days, stirring daily. After that strain into fermenting jar or bottle and fit an airlock, and move into a temperature of about 17°C. After another two months the ferment will probably have finished; when the wine has cleared, siphon it off into clean bottles. It is best kept at least a year from the date of making but can well be sampled within six months – and no doubt will be!

* Maize wine (medium)

	Ingredients	Metric	British	USA
	Crushed maize	¾ kilo	1 lb	¾ lb
	Demerara sugar	1 ½ kilos	3 lb	2 ½ lb
	Sweet oranges	4	4	4
	Lemon	1	1	1
	Raisins	½ kilo	1 lb	¾ lb
or	Concentrate (white)	280 ml	½ pint	½ pint
	Amylozyme	As directed		
	Water	4.5 litres	1 gallon	1 gallon
	Yeast and nutrient			
	Campden tablet	1	1	1

Despite the amount of sugar, this will make a medium wine. It is a help to soak the maize overnight in some of the water to soften it, and then, when you come to make your wine, run it through a coarse mincer, together with the raisins. A cupful of grape concentrate can be substituted for the raisins. Peel the lemon and oranges, being careful to miss the white pith, and put the rinds into a polythene bucket with the sugar, maize, raisins, and the juice of the fruits. Pour over the ingredients the water, which need be only hot (not boiling) add one crushed Campden tablet, and stir well to dissolve it and the sugar. It helps the clarity of the wine to add Amylozyme enzyme at this stage. Allow the liquor to cool to 21°C, then add the yeast and yeast nutrient and keep the bucket in a warm place, closely covered, for 10 days, stirring well each day. Then strain into fermenting jar or bottle and fit an airlock.

* Prune wine (sweet)

Ingredients	Metric	British	USA
Prunes	1 kilo	2 lb	1 ¾ lb
Grape concentrate (white)	140 ml	¼ pint	¼ pint
Sugar	1 ½ kilos	3 ¼ lb	2 ¾ lb
Campden tablet	1	1	1
Water	4.5 litres	1 gallon	1 gallon
Yeast and nutrient			
Pectic enzyme			

Put the prunes in a polythene bucket with the water and enzyme, mashing and stirring them daily for 10 days. Then strain, and either press the pulp or squeeze it by hand to extract as much juice and flavour as possible. Add the sugar, grape concentrate, and a crushed Campden tablet, and stir to dissolve. Then add the yeast and yeast nutrient and leave to ferment in a warm place, as usual, for 10 days. Keep the bucket closely covered and stir daily. Then strain into fermenting jar and fit an airlock, and move into slightly cooler place (about 17°C). After another two months the secondary ferment should be finished and when the wine clears it should be racked off into clean bottles.

January

* Raisin wine (dry)

Ingredients	Metric	British	USA
Large raisins	3½ kilos	8 lb	6½ lb
Citric acid	1 tablesp.	1 tablesp.	1 tablesp.
Campden tablet	1	1	1
Water	4.5 litres	1 gallon	1 gallon
Yeast and nutrient			
Pectic enzyme			

Clean the raisins thoroughly by washing them in a colander, then mince through a coarse mincer. Put them into a fermentation vessel with a wide neck, pour on the cold water, and add one crushed Campden tablet and the pectic enzyme. Keep the jar covered. Two days later add the yeast, acid, and nutrient, and fit an airlock to the jar. Alternatively cover the wide neck with a sheet of polythene secured by a rubber band, which will serve the same purpose. Keep the fermentation jar in a warm place (about 21°C) for a few days, and afterwards in a temperature of about 17°C until the ferment has finished. Each day give the vessel a good shake. When fermentation has finished strain the liquor off the raisins, which can then easily be removed (hence the need for a wide-necked jar, with a narrow-necked one it can be a fiddly business). Put into a fresh jar fitted with a fermentation lock and leave for a further three months before racking (siphoning the wine off the lees) again and bottling.

This wine is quite expensive but by using some sugar or grape concentrate you can reduce the amount of raisins required, although the wine will have nothing like the same body. Here is a recipe, however, using that method.

* Raisin wine (medium)

Ingredients	Metric	British	USA
Large raisins	1 kilo	2 lb	1¾ lb
Sugar	1 kilo	2 lb	1¾ lb
Water	4.5 litres	1 gallon	1 gallon

Citric acid	1 teaspoon	1 teaspoon	1 teaspoon
Yeast and nutrient			
Pectic enzyme			

Mince the raisins, put them in the water, and boil for an hour. Strain the liquor on to the sugar, stir well to dissolve, allow to cool to 21°C and pour into fermenting bottle. Add the pectic enzyme, yeast, acid and nutrient. Keep in a warm place until it begins to clear, then rack for the first time, into a clean jar, re-fitting an airlock. When the fermentation ceases completely siphon into clean bottles and cork.

* Grapefruit wine (dry)

Ingredients	Metric	British	USA
Large grapefruit	6	6	6
White grape concentrate	500 ml	1 pint	1 pint
Sugar	1.3 kilos	3 lb	2½ lb
Water	4.5 litres	1 gallon	1 gallon
Yeast and nutrient			
Campden tablet	1	1	1

Clean the fruit and grate the skins finely. Put the water, concentrate, gratings and juice into a bucket and add 1 Campden tablet. Cover. Twenty-four hours later add the yeast. Stand the bowl in a warm place (21°C is ideal), covered closely, and leave for five or six days, stirring thoroughly twice daily. Strain off the liquor through a nylon sieve and dissolve the sugar in it. Put into fermenting jar, filling to shoulder, and fit an airlock. Put surplus in a separate bottle and use to top up when ferment quietens. Leave to ferment out, and when this has happened rack into clean bottles and cork firmly.

January

* Citrus wine (sweet)

Ingredients	Metric	British	USA
Concentrate (white)	280 ml	½ pint	½ pint
Grapefruit	3	3	3
Lemons	3	3	3
Oranges	3	3	3
Sugar	1.5 kilos	3½ lb	3 lb
Campden tablet	1	1	1
Water	4.5 litres	1 gallon	1 gallon

Firstly peel the fruit (do not squeeze the skins or include any white pith) keeping the peel as intact as possible so that it can be retrieved easily later. Put water into a polythene bucket and add the chopped-up fruit, crushed Campden tablet and sugar, stirring thoroughly to dissolve the latter. Twenty-four hours later add the yeast and yeast nutrient, cover closely, and leave in a warm place (about 21°C) for a fortnight, stirring daily. At the end of this period take out the peel and, having strained off the liquor, squeeze out the fruit pulp and add the resultant juice to the bulk. Put into fermenting jar and fit an airlock, and leave to ferment out. Siphon it into clean bottles when it has done so.

* Date wine (medium)

Ingredients	Metric	British	USA
Dates	1.5 kilos	3 lb	2¼ lb
Sugar	1 kilo	2 lb	1½ lb
Citric acid	1 tablesp.	1 tablesp.	2 tablesps.
Grape tannin	1 teaspoon	1 teaspoon	1 teaspoon
Water	4.5 litres	1 gallon	1 gallon
Yeast and nutrient			
Pectic enzyme			

What better use for dates left over from Christmas! Chop or mince the dates and pour over them the boiling water, in which the sugar has been dissolved. Cover the bucket closely with a heavy cloth and add the other ingredients when cool. Ferment on the pulp for a week and then strain into fermenting jar and fit an airlock, topping up with a little cold water if necessary. Ferment out, rack when clear, and bottle.

* 'Instant wine' (dry) by A. S. Henderson

If you have just started winemaking and want an 8 per cent wine which is suitable for table use, quickly made, rapid to mature, and low-priced, try this 'instant wine' recipe:

Ingredients	Metric	British	USA
Tinned grapefruit juice	500 ml	1 pint	1 pint
Light dried malt (Edme)	250 g	½ lb	½ lb
Sugar	500 g	1 lb	¾ lb
Water	4.5 litres	1 gallon	1 gallon
Yeast and nutrient			

Dissolve the sugar in up to half the water, putting the saucepan over a very low heat to speed up the solution. Meanwhile dissolve the dried malt extract in a little cold water, open the tin of fruit juice, and funnel everything into the fermentation jar. Dissolve the yeast nutrient with a little warm water and add to the jar, top up with cold water to the shoulder (this should reduce the whole to a safe temperature) and add the yeast. Shake well, and fit an airlock. Stand in a warm place and watch it go! Within 24 hours the stream of bubbles should be continuous, not less than one per second.

After a day or two, a thick layer will form on the bottom. Give the jar a swirl round daily to agitate the deposit. When gravity has dropped to 1004, or less (10–14 days), filter. Filter with any good proprietary filter and keep the finished wine a week in a cool place before drinking. Other fruit juices (except, God forbid, tomato!) can be used in the same way.

January

* Jam wine

Ingredients	Metric	British	USA
Any fruit jam (e.g. strawberry, raspberry)	1.5 kilos	3 lb	2½ lb
Sugar	750 g	1½ lb	1 lb
Grape concentrate	100 g	¼ lb	¼ lb
Raisins	225 g	½ lb	½ lb
Citric acid	10 g	1 dessertsp.	1 tablesp.
Pectin destroying enzyme (IMPORTANT)	5 g	1 teaspoon	1 teaspoon
Grape tannin	5 g	1 teaspoon	1 teaspoon
Water	4.5 litres	1 gallon	1 gallon

or (for Raisins)

Pour the boiling water over the jam, in a plastic bucket, and leave to cool. Then add the anti-pectin enzyme and acid and leave for 24 hours. Next, add the minced raisins (or concentrate), sugar, tannin, yeast and yeast nutrient. Stir well to dissolve the sugar, then cover and leave to ferment for five days or so, giving it a stir each day. Then strain the must through a nylon sieve or muslin into a fermentation jar, fit an airlock, and leave to ferment out. When it is finished and the wine is clear, rack into a clean jar for six months' storage, adding a crushed Campden tablet or wine stabiliser to prevent further fermentation. Bottle as required, preferably after another two or three months.

Note that the use of the pectin-destroying enzyme (Pektolase or Pectinol) is most important in this case, since the jam contains a high level of pectin which may otherwise prevent the wine clearing.

* Tinned peach, apricot, or nectarine

Ingredients	Metric	British	USA
Tinned peach slices	500 g	15 ½ oz	19 fl oz
Sugar	675 g	1 ½ lb	1 lb
Malt extract	¼ kilo	½ lb	½ lb
Citric acid	1 teaspoon	1 teaspoon	1 teaspoon
Tannin	½ teaspoon	½ teaspoon	½ teaspoon
Water to:	4.5 litres	1 gallon	1 gallon
Sauternes yeast and nutrient			
Pectic enzyme			

The peaches can be bought in slices in either 500 g, 15 ½ oz or 16 oz tins, as halves in 500 g tins, or labelled 'white peaches' in 500 g tins. One 15 ½ oz or 16 oz tin will make, using the quantities in the recipe, a light dry table wine, but if a fuller-bodied wine is required use two tins of peaches (roughly 2 lb) – they are quite cheap – and increase the sugar to 1.2 kilo, 2 ¾ lb (USA 2 ¼ lb) the citric acid to 2 teaspoons, and the tannin to 1 teaspoon.

Pour any syrup into your fermenting jar, then mash the fruit with a stainless steel spoon. Boil two quarts of water and dissolve the sugar and malt extract in it, then put 'pulp' into polythene bucket and pour the boiling syrup over it. Allow to cool to tepid (21°C) before adding acid, tannin and pectic enzyme. Stir well, cover closely, and leave in a warm place. Next day stir, pour the whole into the fermenting jar with the syrup from the can, and add yeast, nutrient, and enough cold water to bring level of must to just below the shoulder of the jar, leaving room for a 'head'. Fit an airlock and leave in a warm place for 10 days, shaking jar daily to disperse pulp through liquid. Then strain into fresh jar, and top up to bottom of neck with water. Ferment out, racking and bottling as usual. For a sweet wine use a 1.3 kilo (1 lb 12 oz) tin of pulp and 1.4 kilo (3 ¼ lb) of sugar.

February

* Almond wine (medium)

Ingredients	Metric	British	USA
Grape concentrate (white)	280 ml	½ pint	½ pint
or Raisins	500 g	1 lb	1 lb
Almonds	50 g	1½ oz	1½ oz
Sugar	1.5 kilos	2 lb	2¼ lb
Lemons	2	2	2
Water to:	4.5 litres	1 gallon	1 gallon
Yeast and nutrient			

The almonds and raisins should be minced and then boiled gently in the water for about an hour, the concentrate being added for the last five minutes. If you prefer, 500 g of raisins can be boiled with the almonds and the concentrate omitted. Add enough fresh water to make the quantity up to one gallon again. Pour the liquor on to the sugar, stirring well to dissolve, then add the juice and grated rind of the lemons, taking care to include no white pith. Add the yeast and nutrient, when the temperature has dropped to 21°C, and endeavour to maintain roughly that temperature for 10 days, keeping the bucket or bowl closely covered. Then strain the wine through a nylon sieve into the fermenting bottle and fit an airlock. Leave until it begins to clear and then rack.

* Dried elderberry wine (dry) (or sloe)

Ingredients	Metric	British	USA
Dried elderberries	¼ kilo	½ lb	¼ lb
Concentrate (red)	100 ml	¼ pint	¼ pint
Sugar	1.25 kilos	2½ lb	2 lb
Citric acid	1 teaspoon	1 teaspoon	1 teaspoon
Water	4.5 litres	1 gallon	1 gallon
Yeast and nutrient			
Pectic enzyme			

Stir the grape concentrate into the boiling water, with elderberries and the sugar. Stir well to dissolve sugar. Allow to cool, add acid, enzyme, nutrient and yeast. Keep covered in a warm place and stir daily for a week, pushing the fruit down regularly. Strain into fermenting jar, ferment, rack when clear, and bottle. An excellent dry red table wine, best made with a Bordeaux or Pommard yeast. For a sweet wine increase sugar to 3 lb and use a Burgundy yeast.

NB – It is possible to take a second 'run' off the discarded fruit by adding another quota of boiling water, more sugar and grape concentrate, more nutrient and more acid. When it cools, add some of the first batch of fermenting wine as a starter and ferment for 10 days on the pulp, and continue as before. A lighter wine will result.

* Mangold wine (medium)

Ingredients	Metric	British	USA
Mangolds	2.5 kilos	5 lb	3¾ lb
Sugar	1.5 kilos	3 lb	2¼ lb
Lemons	2	2	2
Oranges	2	2	2
Water	4.5 litres	1 gallon	1 gallon
Yeast and nutrient			

Wash the mangolds but do not peel. Cut into pieces and boil until tender. Strain, and to every gallon of liquor add sugar and rinds of oranges and lemons (avoid the white pith) as above, and boil for 20 minutes. Allow the liquor to cool, and add the juice of the oranges and lemons. Stir in the yeast (a general purpose wine yeast or a level teaspoonful of granulated yeast) and leave in a warm place, well covered, for about a week. Then stir, transfer to fermenting bottle or jar, and airlock. When the wine clears, rack it off into a clean storage vessel. Keep it for another six months in a cool place, then bottle.

135

February

* Orange or tangerine wine (medium)

Ingredients	Metric	British	USA
Sweet oranges	12	12	12
Sugar	1.5 kilos	3½ lb	2¾ lb
Water	4.5 litres	1 gallon	1 gallon
Yeast and nutrient			
Pectic enzyme			

Peel six of the oranges thinly, avoiding the white pith like the plague (it imparts a most bitter taste to the wine). Pour a litre (quart) of boiling water on to the rind and allow to stand for 24 hours, then strain off the water into a polythene bucket containing 3 litres of water and the sugar. Cut all the oranges in half and squeeze the juice into the bowl. Stir until the sugar is dissolved, and then add the yeast, nutrient and pectic enzyme. If you use a general purpose wine yeast, which is to be recommended, the liquor can safely be strained from the bucket into a fermenting jar, and fitted with an airlock, within two or three days. Siphon it off the lees for the first time when it clears, and re-bottle two or three months later.

* Seville orange wine (sweet)

Ingredients	Metric	British	USA
Thin-skinned Seville oranges	12	12	10
Lemons	2	2	2
Sugar	2 kilos	4 lb	3 lb
Water	4.5 litres	1 gallon	1 gallon
Yeast and nutrient			
Pectic enzyme			

Peel 6 of the oranges, and throw away the peel. Cut up all the oranges and lemons into slices and put in a fermenting bin with the sugar. Boil the water and pour it on, boiling. Place the fermenter in a moderately warm corner, cover, and when tepid add the nutrient, enzyme, and wine yeast or a teaspoonful of granulated yeast; stir each day for a fortnight. Strain into a gallon jar, filling it up to the top. Put the surplus in a dark bottle and use this for filling up the large jar after racking. Ferment to completion under airlock, rack when it clears, and bottle two months later.

* Coffee wine (dry)

Ingredients	Metric	British	USA
Instant coffee (Nescafé)	15 g	1 level tablesp.	2 tablesps.
Sugar	1 kilo	2¼ lb	1½ lb
Citric acid	15 g	1 tablesp.	2 tablesps.
Water to:	4.5 litres	1 gallon	1 gallon
Ammonium phosphate	1 teaspoon	1 teaspoon	1 teaspoon

Put coffee, sugar, citric acid and ammonium phosphate in mixing bowl and pour on 2 litres (4 pints) of boiling water. Stir well. Allow to cool, pour into fermenting jar, top up with warm water to shoulder, introduce yeast. Fit an airlock. After five days top up with water to bottom of neck, refit an airlock, ferment out, rack and bottle as usual.

* Parsnip sherry (oloroso)

Ingredients	Metric	British	USA
Parsnips	2 kilos	4½ lb	4½ lb
Hops	20 g	½ oz	½ oz
Malt extract	250 g	½ lb	½ lb
Light brown sugar	1.5 kilo	3¼ lb	2½ lb
Gravy browning (liquid)	5 ml	1 teaspoon	1 teaspoon
Citric acid	12 g	2 teaspoons	2 teaspoons
Water	4.5 litres	1 gallon	1 gallon
Yeast and nutrient			
Pectic enzyme			

Clean parsnips, but do not peel, and ensure that their weight is not less than 4 lb after cleaning. Cut them into slices and boil gently in half the water until soft (but not mushy, or the wine will not clear). Then strain into a pan. Put the hops in a bag in the remaining water and boil gently for half an hour, then stir in the gravy browning (which is only caramel colouring). Mix the liquids together and stir in the malt, sugar, citric acid; and allow to cool to blood heat, and then add yeast nutrient and pectic enzyme. Keep warm and closely covered and ferment for 14 days, then stir, siphon into fermenting jar and fit an airlock. When the wine clears siphon off into sterilised bottles and keep for a further six months.

* Banana wine

Ingredients	Metric	British	USA
Peeled bananas	2 kilos	4 lb	3 lb
Banana skins	¼ kilo	½ lb	½ lb
Grape concentrate (white)	100 ml	¼ lb	¼ lb
Lemon	1	1	1
Orange	1	1	1
Sugar	1.5 kilos	3 lb	2¼ lb
Water	4.5 litres	1 gallon	1 gallon
Yeast and nutrient			
Amylozyme			

Use black or spotted bananas, whatever you can scrounge. Place bananas and fruit peel into a cloth bag and put the bag, tied up, into a large saucepan or boiler with the water. Bring to the boil, then gently simmer for half an hour. Pour the hot liquor over the sugar and fruit juice, and when the cloth bag has cooled squeeze it with the hands to extract as much liquor as possible. When all the liquor is lukewarm 21°C add the Amylozyme and, 24 hours later, the yeast. Cover closely. Leave it in a warm place for a week, stirring daily, then pour into a glass jar and move to a cooler place; it will be a thick-looking mess, like a lot of soapsuds. Keep the jar closed with a piece of clingfilm and a rubber band, or stopper it with cotton wool (so that it can easily be cleaned in case of foaming over), and in a couple of months it will have a large sediment at the bottom. Siphon off, then add the grape concentrate. Fit an airlock and siphon off again after four months; by then it will have started to clear. Leave a further six months before sampling. It improves the longer you keep it.

Birch sap wine

This is a wine which, intriguing by its novelty, is also an excellent wine in its own right. It is probably of Baltic origin and during the last century was a popular drink in Russia, so much so that upon occasions whole forests of young birch trees were killed by the peasantry, who tapped them too enthusiastically . . . so beware of that error. No harm will come to a tree by the loss of a gallon or so of sap in the spring (about the first fortnight in March) but the hole must afterwards be plugged with a wooden plug, and can then be used again next year. I am also told, although I can produce no written authority for it, that birch sap wine was a favourite with Albert, the Prince Consort, who doubtless had plenty of trees at his disposal!

The main precautions to observe are that you do not tap a very young tree – it should be at least 9 in diameter – that you bore only far enough into the tree for your tap or tube to be held securely (bore to just beyond the inside of the bark where the sap rises and not into the 'dead wood' of the centre of the trunk), that you do not take more than a gallon of sap from one tree, and that you plug the hole afterwards. Neglect of any of these points may harm the tree.

Ingredients	Metric	British	USA
Birch sap	4.5 litres	1 gallon	1 gallon
Lemons	2	2	2
Sweet oranges	1	1	1
Concentrate (white)	280 ml	½ pint	½ pint
Sugar	1.5 kilos	3 lb	2¼ lb
Seville orange	1	1	1
Yeast and nutrient			

Obtain a wooden beer or wine-barrel tap, or a piece of glass or plastic tubing, fixed in a bung or cork. With a brace and bit of the same diameter as tap or bung bore a hole into the trunk of the tree to just beyond the

March

inside of the bark, and insert the tube, which should incline slightly downwards to allow the sap to run easily. In March, when the sap is rising, it should be possible to draw off a gallon or so of liquor in two or three days. Plug the hole afterwards.

Peel the oranges and lemons (discard all white pith) and boil the peel in the sap for 20 minutes. Add enough water to restore the volume of one gallon, then pour into a bucket containing the sugar and concentrate. Stir until sugar is dissolved; when the liquor has cooled to 21°C add the fruit juice and yeast. Cover the bucket with a thick cloth and keep in a warm place until fermentation has quietened. Then strain into fermenting jar and fit an airlock. Leave until fermentation ends, then add a crushed Campden tablet, and a level teaspoonful of potassium sorbate or a stabilising tablet. Rack and bottle. Store the bottles on their sides for at least another six months before sampling.

Sycamore and walnut sap wines can be made in the same manner and an excellent beer can be produced by reducing the sugar to 1 lb.

* Pineapple wine (sweet)

Ingredients	Metric	British	USA
Pineapples	4	4	4
Sugar	1.75 kilos	3½ lb	2¾ lb
Citric acid	10 g	2 teaspoons	2 teaspoons
Water	4.5 litres	1 gallon	1 gallon
Yeast and nutrient			

'Top and bottom' the pineapples, then slice them into a 1-gallon saucepan and cover with a third of the water. Bring to boil, and simmer for 25 minutes. Strain on to sugar in a fermenting bin, and add remaining two-thirds of water, cold. Add the citric acid. Stir well to dissolve sugar thoroughly, and leave to cool to blood heat. Then add a wine yeast (preferably from a starter bottle), and a yeast nutrient if desired. (I use a general purpose wine yeast and a teaspoonful of a proprietary nutrient.) Cover the bin closely for a week and leave it in a warm place, giving a daily stir, and then transfer to fermenting jars or bottles, which should be filled to the bottom of the neck and fitted with airlocks. Keep in temperature of about 15°C until the wine begins to clear and has thrown a substantial sediment, then siphon off into clean jars. Then add a crushed Campden tablet, and a level teaspoonful of potassium sorbate or a stabilising tablet. Allow it to throw a fresh sediment, then siphon off into clean bottles and cork. This is a delicious light wine with a delightful bouquet.

Pineapple liqueur

Buy a big juicy pineapple and try your hand at making this really delightful liqueur. Slice the pineapple thinly, sprinkle with a little sugar, and leave for 24 hours. Press out the juice, measure it, and add an equal amount of brandy to which sugar has been added in the proportion of 2 oz sugar to every half pint of brandy. Put in a jar with a few slices of fresh pineapple and leave for three weeks, then strain and bottle.

* Rice and raisin (medium)

Ingredients	Metric	British	USA
Raisins	1.5 kilos	3 lb	2 ¼ lb
Rice (long grain)	2.25 kilos	5 lb	3 ¾ lb
Sugar	4.5 kilos	10 lb	7 ½ lb
Citric acid	2 tablesp.	2 tablesp.	2 serving spoons
Yeast and nutrient	50 g	2 oz	2 oz
Water	13.5 litres	3 gallons	3 gallons

Dissolve sugar in some heated water taken from the 3 gallons. Allow to cool and pour over rice and raisins (do not chop or mince the raisins). Then add the acid and remaining water and sprinkle on yeast and nutrient. Stir and leave in a warm place. Stir daily for 21 days then strain through a fine sieve into three 4.5 litre (1 gallon) jars. Fit airlocks to the jars and keep them in a warm place until fermentation stops. Then filter the wine through one of the popular filters and it is then ready for drinking straight away. If it is not drunk within 2 months add 1 Campden tablet per gallon and leave for 9 months.

March

Do not discard the pulp as it can be used to make a lighter wine. Dissolve 3.5 kilos (8 lb) of sugar in 4.5 litres (1 gallon) of hot water and pour on to the rice and raisin residue. Add 6.7 litres (1½ gallons) of cold water plus 30 g (1 oz) citric acid together with fresh yeast. Follow the same procedure as given for the first batch.

* Dried peach wine (sweet)

Ingredients	Metric	British	USA
Dried peaches	1 kilo	2 lb	2 lb
Sugar	1.5 kilos	3½ lb	2¾ lb
Citric acid	10 g	1 dessertsp.	1 tablesp.
Water	4.5 litres	1 gallon	1 gallon
Yeast and nutrient			
Pectic enzyme			

Soak the peaches for 12 hours in the cold water, then place all in a large saucepan or preserving pan, bring to the boil, and simmer for five or six minutes. Strain the liquid off into a polythene bucket, add the sugar, yeast nutrient and enzyme and stir well until all is dissolved. Allow to cool to about 21°C, then add the acid and a general-purpose wine yeast starter or a level teaspoonful of granulated yeast. Cover the bucket closely and keep it in a temperature of 21–24°C for four days, giving it a daily stir; then stir, transfer to fermenting jar, and fit an airlock. When wine clears and fermentation has finished, siphon it off the sediment into clean bottles and cork securely.

* White vin ordinaire (dry)

Ingredients	Metric	British	USA
Canned orange juice	280 ml	½ pint	10 fl oz
Canned pineapple juice	280 ml	½ pint	10 fl oz
Sugar	1 kilo	2 lb	1½ lb
Water	4.5 litres	1 gallon	1 gallon
Bordeaux yeast			
Pectic enzyme			

The sugar is poured into a 4.5 litre jar, the juices and nutrients, etc., are added and the jar is topped up to the shoulder with cold water. Vigorous stirring will dissolve the sugar and the yeast starter and Pectolase are added immediately. This wine will ferment out to dryness in about 3 – 4 weeks at 21°C. At the end of this time two Campden tablet should be added and the wine racked a week later. After 3 – 4 months the wine is brilliantly clear and is drinkable as a rough white wine but is much improved if cask matured for two months.

* Red vin ordinaire (dry)

Ingredients	Metric	British	USA
Dried elderberries	100 g	¼ lb	¼ lb
Concentrate (red)	280 ml	½ pint	½ pint
Sugar	750 g	1½ lb	1¼ lb
Citric acid	2 teaspoons	1 dessertsp.	1 tablesp.
Water	4.5 litres	1 gallon	1 gallon
Burgundy yeast and nutrient			
Pectic enzyme			

The ingredients are crushed and placed in a bucket and boiling water is poured over them. The water level is brought up to 1 gallon and when cool the yeast starter and Pectolase are added. The 'pulp' is strained off after four days and therefore the fermentation continues in a 4.5 litre jar. Rack when all sugar has been used up (generally within a month) and allow to clear.

143

April

* Agrimony wine (medium)

Ingredients	Metric	British	USA
Agrimony	1 litre	2 pints	2 pints
Sugar	1 kg	2¼ lb	2 lb
Sultanas	455 g	1 lb	½ lb
Tannin	½ teaspoon	½ teaspoon	½ teaspoon
Ammonium phosphate	1½ teaspoon	1 teaspoon	
Citric acid	⅛ teaspoon	⅛ teaspoon	⅛ teaspoon
Malic acid	¼ teaspoon	¼ teaspoon	¼ teaspoon
Tartaric acid	¼ teaspoon	¼ teaspoon	¼ teaspoon
Water	4.5 litres	1 gallon	1 gallon
Lactose	30 g	1 oz	1 oz

Wash the agrimony in cold running water, put in a plastic bucket, and pour over 2.3 litres (4 pints) of boiling water. Cover; leave for three days, stirring twice daily. Put the sugar and chopped sultanas into another bucket, and pour 2.3 litres (4 pints) of boiling water over them; add the tannin (or ½ pint tea), the acids, and the liquor (strained through muslin) in which the agrimony has been soaking; stir to dissolve the sugar. When cooled to 21°C, add the yeast and the phosphate, stirring to dissolve. Cover with linen sheeting, and keep at this temperature for 7 days, stirring three times daily. Strain through muslin into another bucket, and then siphon off into a fermentation jar, fit an airlock, and ferment out. If a yeast deposit occurs, siphon into a clean fermentation jar three times, at monthly intervals. Bottle when the wine has been six months in the making, adding the lactose solution.

Bees wine

"You used to stand it in the window, and the bees used to go up and down in the liquid . . . it made quite a pleasant drink." When you hear someone saying this they are quite certainly talking about that old novelty, 'bees wine', otherwise known as Palestinian or Californian Bees or Balm of Gilead. Actually the 'bees' are merely a certain type of yeast (or rather a mixture of yeasts and bacteria) which has clumping properties – hence its name, *Saccharomyces pyriformis.*

As the clumps of yeast form, the carbon dioxide which is given off during fermentation carries them to the surface, where the bubbles disperse and allow the clumps to sink to the bottom again. The yeast clumps thus move up and down and are rather like 'busy little bees'. Presumably 'standing the jar on the windowsill' allowed it to get some sunshine, and therefore warmth to speed the fermentation, as well as light to show off the movement of the 'bees'.

Nowadays it is quite difficult to obtain a culture, the only source of which I know being Roy Ekins, 4 Lytles Close, Formby, Liverpool L37 4BT, who can supply cultures, for experimental purposes only, for £2 plus 50p p&p. Please note that under the present legislation these cultures cannot be sold as a food-grade or beverage-producing culture.

To my mind bees wine is more of a novelty than a means of producing anything of which a true wine buff could be proud, but if you wish to try your hand at bees wine here is the recipe:

Dissolve about 2 oz of brown sugar in one pint of cold water in a cylindrical, wide-mouthed jar – a Kilner jar or similar vessel will do – pop in your 'bees'. Add a pinch of citric acid, and a little yeast nutrient and cover the jar with a cloth. Each day for a week add 1 teaspoon of sugar and 1 teaspoon of ground ginger. Then dissolve 3 ½ teacups of sugar in 4 teacups of boiling water, and make up to five pints with cold water. Add a teaspoon of citric acid, and strain the liquid from the 'bees' into the syrup, stirring the bulk well as you do so. Bottle your bees wine in screw-stoppered bottles but leave the stoppers loose for three hours, then screw down. The bees wine should be ready to drink in a fortnight. The 'bees' themselves will have doubled in quantity, so they can be halved, and each portion used to start a new batch. The culture can also be used in place of the yeast in ginger beer recipes. However, as it does not ferment very strongly, do not make more than two pints at a time with the contents of a tube culture. After a few fermentations, the culture will, of course, have multiplied considerably, and can then be used for larger batches.

An alternative recipe is:

(a)   Dissolve 2 oz demerara sugar in warm water and make up to one pint. Add a teaspoonful of black treacle and a level teaspoonful (not more) of powdered ginger.

145

April

(b)   Put the solution into a suitable wide-mouthed container such as a Kilner jar or 2 lb jam jar.

(c)   Add the culture of bees.

(d)   Cover with a clean handkerchief held in place with a rubber band.

(e)   Keep the container in a warm light room. A sunny windowsill is ideal. Fermentation will take place and the number of bees will increase.

(f)   On alternate days, add two rounded teaspoonfuls of demerara sugar until the fermentation has been going for 8–10 days.

(g)   Strain the bees from the wine.

(h)   Leave the wine in a cool place for a day or two to settle.

(i)   The wine may now be consumed directly, or kept in bottles in the cold for a week or two before it is used.

Flower wines

April is the month for starting to make some of the delightful light but wonderfully perfumed flower wines that are possible, but it should be noted that some wild flowers (e.g. cowslip) are becoming scarce and perhaps should not be picked in quantity. Many are protected by law, and must not be uprooted. But flowers which are plentiful make delightful wines.

* Primrose wine

Ingredients	Metric	British	USA
Primroses	4.5 litres	1 gallon	1 gallon
Sugar	1.5 kilos	3 lb	2½ lb
Oranges	2	2	2
Lemon	1	1	1
Grape tannin	1 teaspoon	1 teaspoon	1 teaspoon
Water	4.5 litres	1 gallon	1 gallon
Yeast and nutrient			

Bring the water to the boil and stir into it the sugar, making sure that it is all dissolved. Put the peel of the oranges and lemon into a crock, bowl or polythene bucket, being careful to exclude all white pith, to prevent the wine from having a bitter taste, and pour the hot syrup over the rinds. Allow to cool to 21°C, then add the flowers, the fruit juice, tannin, your chosen yeast, and some yeast nutrient. Cover closely and leave for five days in a warm place, stirring each day. Then strain through a nylon sieve or muslin into a fermenting jar, filling it to the bottom of the neck, and fit an airlock. Leave for three months, then siphon the wine off the yeast deposit into a fresh jar. A further racking after another three months is helpful, and shortly after that the wine will be fit to drink, if still young.

Gorse wine (sweet)

Later in the month, and right up till July, you can make another flower wine which is thought by many of be one of the most agreeable social wines, gorse.

Ingredients	Metric	British	USA
Gorse flowers	4.5 litres	1 gallon	1 gallon
Sugar	1.5 kilos	3 lb	2½ lb
Oranges	2	2	2
Lemons	2	2	2
Grape tannin	1 teaspoon	1 teaspoon	1 teaspoon
Water	4.5 litres	1 gallon	1 gallon
Yeast and nutrient			

The best plan is to put your flowers in a netting bag, which can then be dropped into the water and simmered for a quarter of an hour, afterwards making up the water to the original quantity. When you remove the bag, squeeze it well to extract the liquor, and return this to the bulk. Then dissolve the sugar in the liquid, and add the lemon and orange juice, and the skins (no pith) of the fruit. Allow the liquor to cool to 21°C, then add the tannin, general-purpose wine yeast, or a level teaspoon of granulated yeast, and yeast nutrient. Three days is sufficient for fermentation to get well under way, as long as the liquor is kept in a warm place 17–21°C, closely covered, and given an occasional stir. Then strain it into a fermenting jar and fit an airlock and put in a slightly cooler place. Siphon it off the lees when the top third has cleared (after two or three months) and again three months later. Put in a cooler place still, 13°C; it will be ready to drink after another two months or so.

Coltsfoot wine (sweet)

Coltsfoot grows abundantly in the British Isles but the flowers are not always easy to come by in quantity unless you have previously earmarked the plant's position. It is usually to be found in waysides, railway embankments and waste places, the bright yellow flowers putting in an appearance from March onwards, long in advance of the heart-shaped leaves. Because of this the old country name for this plant was 'Son Before Father!' (Those who do not live in the country can obtain the dried flowers from a herbalist. One small packet will make a gallon.)

Ingredients	Metric	British	USA
Coltsfoot flowers	4.5 litres	1 gallon	1 gallon
Sugar	1.5 kilos	3 lb	2½ lb
Oranges	2	2	2
Lemons	2	2	2
Grape tannin	1 teaspoon	1 teaspoon	1 teaspoon
Water	4.5 litres	1 gallon	1 gallon
Yeast and nutrient			

Dissolve the sugar in the water and bring to the boil. Simmer for five minutes. Remove from the heat and allow to cool. Peel the oranges and lemons thinly, and put the rind into a bowl or stone jar with the juice, tannin and the flowers (just the heads). Pour over the cold syrup, and stir. Add the yeast mixed with a little of the lukewarm liquid and leave to ferment for seven days in a warm place, well covered. Stir daily. Strain into a fermenting jar, cover, or insert an airlock. When fermentation ceases, add one crushed Campden tablet, siphon off and bottle.

* Dandelion wine (1) (medium)

Ingredients	Metric	British	USA
Dandelions	3 litres	3 quarts	3 quarts
Sugar	1.5 kilos	3 lb	2½ lb
Lemons	2	2	2
Orange	1	1	1
Raisins	500 g	1 lb	¾ lb
or Concentrate (white)	280 ml	½ pint	½ pint
Grape tannin	1 teaspoon	1 teaspoon	1 teaspoon
Water	4.5 litres	1 gallon	1 gallon
Yeast and nutrient			

A quart of dandelion heads weighs 225 g (½ lb) and a quart of petals alone 340 g (¾ lb).

The flowers must be freshly gathered (traditionally St George's Day, April 23rd, is the correct occasion), picked off their stalks, and put into a polythene bucket. You do not need to pick off the petals: use the whole heads. Bring the water to the boil, pour over the dandelions, and leave for two days, stirring each day. Keep the bucket closely covered. On the third day, turn all into a boiler, add the sugar and the rinds only of the lemons and orange. Boil for ten minutes. Return to the bucket, and add the juice and 'pulp' of the lemons and orange. Allow to stand till cool, then add wine yeast and the tannin, and yeast nutrient, since this is a liquor likely to be deficient in desirable elements. Let it remain closely covered for three days in a warm place, then strain into fermenting bottles and add the concentrate. Fit traps. Leave until fermentation ceases and rack and top up when wine clears. This wine, made in April or early May, is ready for drinking by Christmas, but improves vastly by being kept a further six months.

May

* Dandelion wine (2) (medium)

Ingredients	Metric	British	USA
Dandelions	2 litres	2 quarts	2 quarts
Sugar	1.5 kilos	3 lb	2½ lb
Oranges	4	4	4
Water	4.5 litres	1 gallon	1 gallon
Yeast and nutrient			

This recipe makes a pleasant alternative to the foregoing one. It is important that the flowers should be picked in sunshine, or at midday, when they are fully opened, and the making of the wine should be done immediately.

Measure the yellow heads, discarding as much green as posible (without being too fussy about it), bringing the water to the boil meanwhile.

Two quarts of whole flower heads weigh 450 g (1 lb). Pour the boiling water over the flowers and leave them to steep for two days. Again, be careful not to exceed this time or a curious odour often invades and spoils what is a most pleasant table wine, properly made. Boil the mixture for 10 minutes with the orange peel (no white pith) and strain through muslin on to the sugar, stirring to dissolve it. When cool add the yeast nutrient, fruit juice and yeast. Put into fermentation jar and fit an airlock, and siphon off into clean bottles when the wine has cleared. It will be just right for drinking with your Christmas poultry!

* Farmhouse tea and raisin wine (medium)

Ingredients	Metric	British	USA
Raisins (large)	1 kilo	2 lb	1½ lb
Wheat	500 g	1 lb	¾ lb
Tea	25 g	1 oz	1 oz
Sugar	1 kilo	2 lb	1½ lb
Citric acid	10 g	1 tablesp.	1 serving spoon
Water	4.5 litres	1 gallon	1 gallon
Yeast and nutrient			

Tie the tea loosely in a muslin bag. Pour the boiling water over it and let it mash, leaving it in the liquor until it is lukewarm. Remove the bag, and to the liquor add the chopped raisins (or 560 ml of white grape concentrate), wheat, sugar and citric acid. Add a Campden tablet. Dissolve one teaspoon of granulated yeast in the liquid and stir it in. Leave it to ferment in a closely-covered fermenting bucket for 21 days, stirring often, then strain into fermenting bottle, top up to bottom of neck, and fit an airlock. Siphon off into clean bottles when fermentation has ceased.

* Tea wine (dry)

Ingredients	Metric	British	USA
Tea	4 tablesp.	4 tablesp.	6 tablesp.
Sugar	1.25 kilos	2½ lb	2 lb
Citric acid	2 teaspoons	2 teaspoons	3 teaspoons
Water	4.5 litres	1 gallon	1 gallon
Yeast and nutrient			

Some of the scented Indian and China teas make lovely wines. Pour the boiling water over the tea and sugar, stir well, and infuse until cool. Strain into fermenting jar, add acid, nutrient and yeast, and top up to bottom of neck with cold water. Fit an airlock, ferment out, and rack and bottle as usual when stable. A clear, dry wine excellent for blending purposes.

Rhubarb wine (medium)

Rhubarb, it is true, *does* contain oxalic acid, which is poisonous, but it is largely confined to the leaves (which we do not use) and not the stems. The acidity of rhubarb is very high but it is possible to make excellent light wines if you keep the fruit content low and employ the 'dry sugar' method of juice extraction. The wine is best made in May with young rhubarb; at other times of the year jellification sometimes seems to occur.

151

May

Ingredients	Metric	British	USA
Rhubarb	1.25 kilos	3 lb	2½ lb
Sugar	1.25 kilos	3 lb	2½ lb
Water to:	4.5 litres	1 gallon	1 gallon
Wine yeast and nutrient			

Reducing the sugar used by ¼ lb and including 250 ml of grape concentrate instead results in a smoother wine, in my experience.

Do not peel the rhubarb but chop it, or slice it thinly. Cover the fruit with the dry sugar and leave it until most of the sugar has dissolved (at least 24 hours) then strain off. Stir the pulp in a little water and strain again, and with more water rinse out all remaining sugar into the liquor, and make up to 1 gallon with water. Add a good general-purpose wine yeast, and the usual nutrients. If you wish to preserve the rhubarb taste ferment on, but if you wish to make a wine tasting rather like hock add one crushed Campden tablet first.

This is an excellent wine for blending, since it will take up the flavour of any other and its own will be virtually lost.

* Mead (dry)

Ingredients	Metric	British	USA
English honey	2 kilos	4 lb	4 lb
Orange	1	1	1
Lemon	1	1	1
Water	4.5 litres	1 gallon	1 gallon
Yeast and nutrient			
Pectic enzyme			

Put the honey into the water and bring to simmering point, skim, then pour into a bucket and allow to cool. Add the juice from the orange and lemon, and the yeast, such as an all-purpose wine yeast, and nutrient.

NB. It is most important to add a good nutrient, since the honey is deficient in essential minerals. Pour into fermentation vessel and fit an airlock. Allow to ferment to completion – this is liable to take much longer than with most country wines – and rack when no further bubbles are passing. Mead should preferably be matured for at least a year after this, but you need to be very strong-willed to follow this advice!

Florida orange wine (dry)

Bill Elks of Luton Amateur Winemakers recommended the following recipe which has proved successful both competitively and socially.

Ingredients	Metric	British	USA
One can Birds Eye Florida Orange (to make 1 pint drinking juice)			
Sugar	900 g	2 lb	1½ lb
Tartaric acid	1 teaspoon	1 teaspoon	1 teaspoon
Pectolase	1 teaspoon	1 teaspoon	1 teaspoon
Tannin	1 g	¼ teaspoon	¼ teaspoon
Nutrient and wine yeast			
Water to:	4.5 litres	1 gallon	1 gallon

Add the orange juice, sugar and nutrient to 2.36 litres (4 pints) of water in a demijohn and stir to dissolve. Dissolve tannin in small amount of boiling water and add to must, top up to 4 litres (7 pints) with cold water, add pectic enzyme and yeast. Ferment under airlock for one week, top up to 4.5 litres (1 gallon) and ferment on to SG 0.995 or below. Rack and bottle after a further two weeks. This wine is fit to drink immediately but improves with keeping and is at its best served chilled.

For a medium social wine add 140 ml (¼ pint) grape concentrate, 225 g (½ lb) sugar and 3 g (¼ teaspoon) tartaric acid to the above ingredients and proceed as before.

153

May

* Hawthorn blossom wine (sweet)

Ingredients	Metric	British	USA
Hawthorn blossom	2.25 kilos	2 quarts	4 pints
Sugar	1.5 kilos	3½ lb	2¾ lb
Lemons	2	2	2
Grape tannin	1 teaspoon	1 teaspoon	1 teaspoon
Water	4.5 litres	1 gallon	1 gallon
Yeast and nutrient			

Grate the rind from the lemons, being careful to include no white pith, and boil with the sugar and the juice of one lemon in the water for half an hour. Pour into a polythene bucket and when it has cooled to 21°C add the yeast (and, preferably, as with all flower wines, a good yeast nutrient). Leave for 24 hours, then tip in the flowers. Let the mixture stand for another eight days, stirring well each day, and keeping the bucket closely covered. Then strain through your sieve into fermenting vessel, and fit an airlock. Rack for the first time when it clears and after a second racking about three months later (about six months in all) bottle in the usual way. This is a light and delicious wine.

* Lemon thyme wine (medium) (By Mr L. Foest, Penygraig House, Ammanford, Carns.)

Ingredients	Metric	British	USA
Lemon thyme leaves	500 ml	1 pint	1 pint
Raisins	500 g	1 lb	¾ lb
or Concentrate (white)	280 ml	½ pint	½ pint
Sugar	1.5 kilos	3 lb	2¼ lb
Rhubarb	1.5 kilos	3 lb	2¼ lb
Water	4.5 litres	1 gallon	1 gallon
Yeast and nutrient			

Cut up the rhubarb into ½ in. lengths, and chop the lemon thyme (to approximately the size of mint when making mint sauce). Pour boiling water over them, then add the raisins or concentrate. Stir every day for two weeks. Strain on to the sugar, stir thoroughly and add yeast, wine yeast, or a level teaspoonful of granulated yeast. Leave to ferment, closely covered and in a warm place, for another two weeks. Strain into fermenting vessel and fit an airlock, and leave until it has fermented right out. You may prefer to add ½ lb – 1 lb more sugar to obtain a much sweeter wine, but this is best done finally, to taste, and not at the outset.

* Nettle wine (sweet)

Ingredients	Metric	British	USA
Young nettle tops	2 litres	2 quarts	4 pints
Sugar	1.5 kilos	3 lb	2½ lb
Lemons	2	2	2
Root ginger	10 g	½ oz	½ oz
Water	4.5 litres	1 gallon	1 gallon

Pick only the tops of the nettles, rinse them in water, and drain. Simmer them in some of the water with the bruised ginger and lemon peel (being careful to exclude any white pith) for 45 minutes. Strain, and make the liquor up to 4.5 litres (1 gallon) by adding more water. Pour this hot liquor over the sugar, add the juice of the lemons and the yeast nutrient, and stir until the sugar dissolves, and when the liquor has cooled to 21°C add the yeast, preferably a general-purpose wine yeast. Keep the bucket closely covered in a warm place, and after four days stir thoroughly and transfer the liquor to fermentation vessel and fit an airlock. When the wine begins to clear, rack off into fresh bottles, and leave for another three months before the final bottling.

Dry sack

Many, out of curiosity, want to try making sack, once a favourite English drink, mentioned by Shakespeare and earlier writers. Some argue that

May

'sack' is a corruption of the Spanish word for dry – 'seco' – but it is more likely that it derives from 'sacke' sherry, which was first shipped to Plymouth from Jerez de la Frontera in the fifteenth century, the name being taken from the Spanish word 'sacar', to export. As a descriptive term, it later came to be applied to mead as well.

This is an adaptation of an old country recipe for making mock sack:

Ingredients	Metric	British	USA
Fennel roots	3 or 4	3 or 4	3 or 4
Sprays of rue	3 or 4	3 or 4	3 or 4
Honey	1.75 kilos	4 lb	3 lb
Citric acid	2 teaspoons	1 dessertsp.	1 tablesp.
Water	9 litres	2 gallons	2 gallons
Yeast and nutrient			

Wash the roots and leaves and boil them in the water for 45 minutes. Do not be tempted to add more fennel or you will get an unpleasantly strong flavour. Then pour the liquor through a nylon sieve and add the honey. Boil the whole for nearly two hours, skimming off any froth or scum which arises. Allow the liquor to cool to 21°C, then add your chosen yeast and yeast nutrient, and put into fermenting jars and fit airlocks. Sack, like most meads, may be a little slow to ferment and mature, and it is important not to omit the yeast nutrient, or this will be aggravated. Rack after four months if the sack has cleared, if not, delay racking until it has. It is fit for drinking after a year.

* Vanilla wine (sweet)

Ingredients	Metric	British	USA
Rhubarb	2.75 kilos	6 lb	5 lb
Sugar	1.75 kilos	4 lb	3 lb
Lemons	2	2	2
Hawthorn blossom	4.5 litres	1 gallon	1 gallon
Water	4.5 litres	1 gallon	1 gallon
Yeast and nutrient			

When boiling water is used in the making of rhubarb wine jellification is often caused later, during fermentation. It is safer, therefore, to employ a cold water method, which also preserves the fragrances of the flowers.

If cold water is used, of course, the natural yeasts present in quantity (the bloom on the rhubarb) may complicate your ferment if you are using a wine yeast and it is therefore best to add a little sulphite (one Campden tablet per gallon) at the outset. Alternatively you may care in this case to ferment with the natural yeast (in this case, since there is so much of it present, the method usually works quite well). If you do, omit the Campden tablet, and add no yeast.

Cut the rhubarb into small pieces, cover with cold water, and add hawthorn flowers and the juice and rind of the two lemons, excluding any white pith. Add also one crushed Campden tablet. Keep the pan closely covered (*not* in a warm place) and stir daily for 10 days. Strain on to 2 lb sugar, stir thoroughly until all sugar is dissolved, and add yeast. Keep in a warm place, closely covered. After four to five days add the remainder of the sugar, stirring thoroughly, then transfer the liquor to fermenting jar and fit an airlock. Siphon off the lees after three months, and again three months later, when the wine may be bottled. At the second racking it will be vastly improved by the addition of a small quantity of glycerine, to counter any over-acidity.

* Balm wine (medium)

Ingredients	Metric	British	USA
Balm leaves (or small packet of dried balm)	2.5 litres	2 quarts	4 pints
Raisins	500 g	1 lb	¾ lb
or Concentrate (white)	280 ml	½ pint	½ pint
Sugar	1.5 kilos	3 lb	2½ lb
Lemon	1	1	1
Orange	1	1	1
Grape tannin	1 teaspoon	1 teaspoon	1 teaspoon
Water	4.5 litres	1 gallon	1 gallon
Yeast and nutrient			

Add boiling water to the bruised leaves, raisins or concentrate, sugar and the juice and rinds of the lemon and orange. When cool add yeast. Allow to work for seven days, then siphon into fermenting vessel with an airlock until fermentation is finished. The tender shoots should be used if aroma is considered of most importance.

Elderflower hock (1)

This makes a delightful white wine of the hock type, but if it turns out slightly too dry for your liking add one or at most two drops of Sweetex per bottle.

Ingredients	Metric	British	USA
Elderblossom (4 – 5 sprays, not pressed down)	300 ml	½ pint (or 2 oz)	½ pint (or 2 oz)
Sugar	1 kilo	2¼ lb	2 lb
White grape concentrate	100 ml	3½ oz	2 oz
Lemons	3	3	3
Grape tannin	¼ teaspoon	¼ teaspoon	¼ teaspoon
Water	4.5 litres	1 gallon	1 gallon
Hock yeast and nutrient			

Trim the flowerlets from the spray with scissors, and put them into your polythene bucket with the sugar, concentrate, and lemon rinds (no pith) and pour 3.5 litres (6 pints) boiling water on to them. Stir to dissolve sugar, and leave till cool, then add the lemon juice, tannin, nutrient and yeast. Leave in a warm place, closely covered, for four days, then strain into fermenting jar, top up to bottom of neck with cold water, and continue as usual.

Ready for drinking by Christmas.

* Elderflower wine (2)

Ingredients	Metric	British	USA
Elderflowers (not pressed down)	500 ml	¾ pint	¾ pint
or ½ oz dried flowers			
Sugar	1.5 kilos	3½ lb	2¾ lb
Raisins	250 g	½ lb	½ lb
or Concentrate (white)	140 ml	¼ pint	¼ pint
Lemons	3	3	2
Grape tannin	1 teaspoon	1 teaspoon	1 teaspoon
Water	4.5 litres	1 gallon	1 gallon

Threequarters of a pint of elderflowers weigh about 3 oz.

Gather the flowers on a sunny day when they are fully opened, and trim them from the stems with a pair of scissors, until you have ¾ pint (pressed down lightly) of petals. Bring the water to the boil and pour over the flowers, then add the sugar, chopped raisins or concentrate and lemon juice. When cool 21°C add the yeast (a prepared wine yeast is best but granulated yeast can be used), your grape tannin, and nutrient. The nutrient is *most* important in this case. Cover well and leave to ferment in a warm place for four or five days. Strain into another jar, fit an airlock, and leave to ferment. When it clears, siphon the wine off the deposit for the first time; two months later rack it again, and bottle it.

Sparkling elderflower

The previous wine will be nearly dry but when it has started to clear, and while there is still some sugar present, it may prove suitable to convert into a sparkling wine. A bottle containing some of the wine is stood in a warm place and lightly plugged with cotton wool. If after a week a slight yeast deposit has formed it is quite safe to transfer all the wine to champagne bottles which are either closed with corks well wired down or by screw caps similar to cider flagons. The bottles are stored on their sides in a cool place, and after six months or so should be sparkling and ready to drink. If, on the other hand, when trying the wine out for its suitability for bottle 159 fermentation, a heavy yeast deposit is noted then fermentation must be continued for a few more days, or even weeks, until there is less sugar in the wine. A further test then should show a smaller yeast deposit, in which case the wine can be bottled and complete its fermentation in the bottle. Bottling a wine which shows a heavy deposit will inevitably lead to burst bottles.

This is a practical method but you may wish to be more precise, in which case we advise you to read *Making Sparkling Wines* by John Restall and Don Hebbs (Nexus Special Interests). Try also the 'Sparkletop' special valved stoppers from Condessa that allow the secondary fermentation yeast to be disgorged without the necessity to freeze the bottle necks, or removing the stoppers.

* Green gooseberry wine (dry)

Ingredients	Metric	British	USA
Ripe green gooseberries	2.7 kilos	6 lb	5 lb
Sugar	1.25 kilos	2½ lb	2 lb
Water	3 – 4 litres	6 – 7 pints	6 – 7 pints
Yeast and nutrient			
Pectic enzyme			

Top, tail and wash the gooseberries, put into large bucket and squeeze by hand until they are pulpy. Add the enzyme and water and allow to stand for three days, well covered, stirring occasionally. Strain through two thicknesses of muslin, and add the sugar, stirring until it is all dissolved, then add yeast and yeast nutrient. Put into fermenting bottle and fit an airlock, leaving until bubbles cease to pass, then rack off and leave to mature, siphoning off the lees again after another six months. Leave for a year before drinking. Indistinguishable from a good hock.

* Wallflower wine (dry)

Ingredients	Metric	British	USA
Wallflower blossoms	500 ml	1 pint	1 pint
Large raisins or sultanas	250 g	½ lb	½ lb
Concentrate (white)	140 ml	¼ pint	¼ pint
Sugar	1.25 kilos	2½ lb	2 lb
Lemons, juice	2	2	2
Grape tannin	1 teaspoon	1 teaspoon	1 teaspoon
Water	4.5 litres	1 gallon	1 gallon
Yeast and nutrient			

or

Put the sugar, minced sultanas, and flowerlets into a polythene bucket and pour over them 3 litres (3 quarts) hot (not boiling) water. Stir vigorously, when cool add the lemon juice, tannin, and a general-purpose wine yeast, and ferment, well covered, for not more than three days. Strain into fermentation jar, top up with cold boiled water to bottom of neck, fit an airlock, and continue as usual. If desired grape concentrate can be substituted for the raisins or sultanas.

* Parsley wine

Ingredients	Metric	British	USA
Parsley, fresh (or 1 small packet dried parsley)	500 g	1 lb	1 lb
Sugar	1.75 kilos	4 lb	3 lb
Oranges	2	2	2
Lemons	2	2	2
Grape tannin	1 teaspoon	1 teaspoon	1 teaspoon
Water	4.5 litres	1 gallon	1 gallon
Yeast and nutrient			

Boil the parsley (the dried variety should firstly be infused for 24 hours), and thinly peeled rinds of the lemons and oranges for 20 minutes in the gallon of water. Strain on to the sugar and stir well. When lukewarm add

161

June

the yeast and the juice of the citrus fruit. Stir and cover, leave for 24 hours. Pour into fermenting jar and insert an airlock. Leave in a warm place to ferment to a finish. Siphon into a storage jar.

* Sage wine (sweet)

Ingredients	Metric	British	USA
Sage leaves	1.75 kilos	4 lb	3 lb
Minced large raisins	3.5 kilos	8 lb	6 lb
or Concentrate (white)	1 litre	2 pints	2 pints
Barley	½ kilo	1 lb	¾ lb
Lemons	2	2	2
Water	4.5 litres	1 gallon	1 gallon
Yeast and nutrient			

Pour the boiling water on to the raisins (or concentrate) and barley and add the chopped leaves of the red sage. Allow to cool and then add the juice of the two lemons and the nutrient and prepared wine yeast or a level teaspoonful of dried yeast. Keep covered, in a warm place, for seven days, stirring daily, then place in a fermentation vessel with an airlock and ferment in the usual way.

Pansy wine (dry)

Using 3 pints (1.5 litres) of flowers, this can be made in the same way as wallflower wine.

* Bramble tip wine

Ingredients	Metric	British	USA
Bramble tips	4.5 litres	1 gallon	1 gallon
Sugar	1.5 kilos	3 lb	2¼ lb
Citric acid	1 teaspoon	1 teaspoon	1 teaspoon
Grape tannin	1 teaspoon	1 teaspoon	1 teaspoon
Water	4.5 litres	1 gallon	1 gallon

Place the tips in a bucket and cover them with boiling water. Leave this to stand overnight, then bring to the boil and simmer gently for a quarter of an hour. Strain on to the sugar, add the yeast when it has cooled, and keep closely covered in a warm place for 10 days. Then pour into fermenting jar and fit an airlock. Leave until wine clears, then siphon off and bottle.

* Oakleaf or walnut wine (sweet)

Ingredients	Metric	British	USA
Oak or walnut leaves	4.5 litres	1 gallon	1 gallon
Sugar	1.5 kilos	3 lb	2 lb
Citric acid	10 g	2 teaspoons	2 teaspoons
Water	4.5 litres	1 gallon	1 gallon
Yeast and nutrient			

Pick the young leaves now, not later when they are heavy in bitter tannins. Bring 4–6 pints of the water to the boil and dissolve the sugar on it; when it clears pour, boiling, over the leaves. Infuse overnight, and next day strain into fermenting jar. Add the citric acid, nutrient and yeast and shake well. Top up to bottom of neck with cold water, and then ferment out in a warm place. Rack when it clears, and again two months later.

* Blackcurrant, redcurrant or whitecurrant wine (medium)

Ingredients	Metric	British	USA
Black-, red- or whitecurrants	1.5 kilos	3 lb	2 ¼ lb
Sugar	1.75 kilos	3 lb	2 ½ lb
Water	4.5 litres	1 gallon	1 gallon
Yeast and nutrient			
Pectic enzyme			

Put the currants into a plastic bucket or bowl and crush them. Boil up the sugar in the water and pour, still boiling, on to the currants. When it has 163

July

cooled to about blood heat, add the pectic enzyme and a day later a wine
yeast, and keep closely covered for five days in a warm place, giving it an
occasional stir. Then strain into a fermenting jar, fit an airlock. Let it stand
until fermentation ceases and the wine clears, usually in about three
months, then siphon off into fresh, sterilised bottles.

Blackcurrant (Ribena) wine

One 12 oz bottle of Ribena Blackcurrant juice will in fact make one gallon
of wine. Dissolve 1.5 kilo (3 lb) of sugar in some warm water, and add the
blackcurrant juice. Bring to the boil and simmer for 10 minutes to drive off
any preservative, cool, and pour into a gallon jar, filling it to the shoulder.
Then add your chosen wine yeast, or a level teaspoon of Allinson's
granulated yeast. The merest trace of acid (one-third of a teaspoon of citric
acid) and a pinch of yeast nutrient should also be added. Insert the airlock
and stand the jar in a warm place for fermentation to get under way. When
the first vigorous fermentation has died down after a fortnight or so, top
up the jar with water to the bottom of the neck, and re-insert the airlock;
then continue with the fermentation in the usual way.

Summer rumpot

This is the time of year to start what the Germans call a rumtopf, or
rumpot, a truly gorgeous idea which, once you have tried it, you will never
fail to repeat each year. All you need is a capacious glazed earthenware jar
with a heavy, well-fitting lid, or some such container. The Germans use
highly-ornamented pots ornamented with fruit and flower designs, so that
it looks attractive on the table, but a plain one does just as well. Mine holds
just over a gallon.

The idea is to use a mixture of soft fruits as they come in season,
and the basic 'recipe' is a pound of fruit, half a pound of sugar, and cover
it a finger's width with Jamaica rum. In our rumpot we use blackcurrants,
redcurrants, strawberries, black cherries, peaches, blackberries and plums,
and one and a half bottles of rum. It scents the whole kitchen when the lid
is lifted, and as for the taste . . . !

We use it as a dessert at Christmas, and if in the unlikely event
of the whole of the contents not having been used up before the next

You can make up your rumpot in one of these attractive jars.

summer, the next year's fruit just goes in on top of the remainder and the rumpot gets going once more. Do try it.

This is the way to pack summer into your pot.

Start with strawberries, the first fruit of the summer. Wash the fruit first and let it dry. Place the fruit in a dish and add the sugar, the quantity should be half the weight of fruit. Leave it for a full hour so the sugar is well absorbed and the flavour extracted. Now put the fruit and any remaining sugar into your rumpot. Pour enough brown Jamaica rum over the fruit to cover it about a finger's width; this means, about ¾ of a bottle of rum on one pound of fruit and a half pound of sugar in the first instance, but much less rum thereafter. If you want to make a particularly good job place a plate over the fruit so the fruit is submerged if the shape of the pot allows it. After that close the pot and put in a cool place. From time to time look to see that there is still enough liquid in the pot. Don't forget there has to be a finger's width of rum over the fruit. If there is not add some more rum.

As soon as the next fruit in season is available do exactly the same as with strawberries, with one difference – for every future pound of fruit add half a pound of sugar, and half a 70 cl bottle of rum, or just enough to keep the fruit covered.

Should you miss the chance to obtain the fruit in fresh form, you can use frozen fruit. Remember that some frozen fruit may have added sugar. The amount will be mentioned on the packet. Make up the sugar to be half the weight of the fruit.

Your Rumpot Calendar

May – June
> One pound strawberries, ½ lb sugar, rum to cover a finger's breadth.

June – July
> One pound of cooking cherries with stones, ½ lb sugar. Enough rum to cover.

July – August
> One pound of apricots or peaches, peeled, destoned and halved, ½ lb sugar. Rum to cover.

August – September
> One pound of blackberries, ½ lb sugar, more rum.
> One pound of plums, destoned, ½ lb sugar, more rum.

October – November
> Pears and/or pineapple, cut up, and any other fruit available, ½ lb sugar, more rum to cover.

After the last inclusion of fruit in November, leave the pot to stand for a few days before trying. It will keep indefinitely.

Broad bean wine (dry)

. . . and you just *must* try this most unusual and astonishing wine. This recipe produces a light dry wine of superb quality, hard as that may be to believe!

	Ingredients	Metric	British	USA
	Broad beans (shelled)	2 kilos	4 lb	3 lb
	Sugar	1.5 kilos	2¾ lb	2 lb
	Raisins	100 g	¼ lb	¼ lb
or	Concentrate (white)	100 ml	4 oz	4 oz
	Citric acid	2 teaspoons	2 teaspoons	2 teaspoons
	Water	4.5 litres	1 gallon	1 gallon
	Yeast and nutrient			

Use beans that are too old for normal culinary purposes. To 2 kilos (4 lb) of shelled beans add 4.5 litres (1 gallon) of water and boil slowly for one hour. It is essential that the skins do not break or you will have difficulty in clearing the wine. Strain off the liquor and make up to 4.5 litres (1 gallon) with boiled water. For a dry wine add 1.4 kilos (2¾ lb) of sugar, the citric acid and 100 g (¼ lb) of raisins or concentrate. When sufficiently cooled add the yeast, and allow five days for the first fermentation. Remove the raisins after this period, fix the airlock and from then on treat as any other wine. By careful use of the hydrometer more sugar can be added at stages, but I do not recommend this as a sweet wine.

* Cherry wine (medium)

Ingredients	Metric	British	USA
Red cherries	2 kilos	4 lb 6 oz	4 lb
Sugar	1.3 kilos	3 lb	2½ lb
Pectin enzyme	1 teaspoon	1 teaspoon	1 teaspoon
Water	4.5 litres	1 gallon	1 gallon
Yeast and nutrient			

Stone the cherries. Crush the fruit in a bowl or polythene bucket and pour over it six pints of water, boiling. Mash well with stainless steel spoon.

July

When cool add the pectic enzyme. Leave for two days, stirring daily, then strain on to sugar and crushed nutrient tablet; stir well. Add yeast, stir well, and leave for 24 hours, closely covered, in a warm place. Then pour into fermenting jar, top up to bottom of neck with cold water, and continue as usual.

* Cherry wine (sweet)

Ingredients	Metric	British	USA
Black cherries	2.75 kilos	6 lb	5 lb
Sugar	2 kilos	4 lb	3 lb
Citric acid	1 teaspoon	1 teaspoon	1 teaspoon
Water	4.5 litres	1 gallon	1 gallon
Yeast and nutrient			

Crush the cherries (without breaking the stones) and then pour the boiling water over them. Leave to soak for 48 hours. Strain through a fine nylon sieve. Bring the juice just to boiling point and pour it over the sugar.

Stir until the sugar is dissolved. Allow to cool and then stir in the yeast and nutrient. Cover closely and ferment in a warm place for 14 days, then put into fermenting bottle and fit an airlock. Siphon off when finished and clear into clean bottles.

* Honeysuckle wine (medium)

Ingredients	Metric	British	USA
Honeysuckle blossom (pressed down lightly)	1 litre	2 pints	2 pints
Sugar	1.5 kilos	3 lb	2¼ lb
Concentrate (white)	100 ml	4 oz	4 oz
Citric acid	2 teaspoons	2 teaspoons	2 teaspoons
Campden tablet	1	1	1
Grape tannin	1 teaspoon	1 teaspoon	1 teaspoon
Water	4.5 litres	1 gallon	1 gallon
Yeast and nutrient			

Honeysuckle berries and foliage are poisonous: the flowers are not. They must be fully open, and dry. Wash them in a colander, pour the water (cold) over them, and stir in 1 kilo of sugar, the minced raisins (or concentrate), and the citrus fruit juice. Add the crushed Campden tablet. Stir well, and next day add the yeast (a Sauternes is suitable), tannin and nutrients. Ferment for a week in a warm place, stirring daily, then add the remaining sugar and stir well. Strain into fermenting jar and ferment, rack and bottle as usual. Use 250 g sugar less for a really dry wine.

* Marigold wine (medium)

Ingredients	Metric	British	USA
Marigold flowers (no stalks)	3 litres	3 quarts	3 quarts
Sugar	1.5 kilos	3 lb	2¼ lb
Lemons	2	2	2
Water	4.5 litres	1 gallon	1 gallon

Bring the water to the boil, dissolve the sugar in it, and allow to cool. Add the crushed flowers, the juice and rind of the lemons (being careful to include no white pith), the yeast nutrient, and yeast (prepared wine yeast or a level teaspoonful of dried yeast). Leave in a warm place, closely covered, for a week, stirring twice daily, then strain into a fermenting jar, insert an airlock, and leave in a fairly warm place to finish. When fermentation ceases and wine has cleared, siphon off into clean bottles and keep in a cool place for at least six months before drinking.

Marrow wine (medium)

Although the recipe which advocates filling a marrow with brown sugar to make Marrow Rum is one which appeals by its novelty I have never yet tasted any made by this method which has been successful, unless the recipe has been considerably adjusted; usually the result is far too sweet. You will find this recipe for marrow wine far more successful.

169

July

Ingredients	Metric	British	USA
Ripe marrow flesh	2.25 kilos	5 lb	4 lb
White sugar (or brown if you wish a rum colour)	1.5 kilos	3 lb	2¼ lb
Citric acid	4 teaspoons	4 teaspoons	4 teaspoons
Oranges	2	2	2
Root ginger	25 g	1 oz	1 oz
Water	4.5 litres	1 gallon	1 gallon
Yeast and nutrient			
Pectic enzyme			

Grate the marrow and use the seeds, slice the oranges, bruise the ginger, and put all into a bucket with the acid. Pour over the boiling water and when cool add enzyme, yeast and nutrient. Leave five days, closely covered, stirring frequently, strain and dissolve the sugar in the liquid. Either put into a fermentation jar and fit an airlock, or keep it closely covered and then ferment in the usual way. When it clears siphon it off the yeast. It should be ready after about six months and can then be bottled.

* Meadowsweet wine (medium)

Ingredients	Metric	British	USA
Meadowsweet flowers heads only or 1 small packet dried heads)	4.5 litres	1 gallon	1 gallon
Sugar	1.5 kilos	3 lb	2¼ lb
Grape tannin	1 teaspoon	1 teaspoon	1 teaspoon
Citric acid	2 teaspoons	1 dessertsp.	1 tablesp.
Raisins	500 g	1 lb	¾ lb
or Concentrate	280 ml	½ pint	½ pint
Water	4.5 litres	1 gallon	1 gallon
Yeast and nutrient			

Place the flowers, chopped fruit and sugar in polythene bucket, pour in the concentrate and boiling water, and stir well. When cool add the citric acid, tannin and yeast nutrient. Introduce the wine yeast and ferment on the pulp for 10 days, stirring twice daily and keeping it closely covered. Then strain into fermentation vessel and ferment, rack, and bottle in due course.

* Morello cherry wine (sweet)

Ingredients	Metric	British	USA
Morello cherries (cracked or windfall)	4 kilos	8 lb	6 lb
Sugar	1.8 kilos	4 lb	3¼ lb
Water	4.5 litres	1 gallon	1 gallon
Yeast and nutrient			
Pectic enzyme			

Stalk and wash the fruit, place in a crock, and add 500 ml (1 pint) of cold water to each 450 g (1 lb) of fruit, and then one crushed Campden tablet and enzyme. Lastly, add a level teaspoonful of dried yeast. Leave for 10 days, keeping closely covered, but stir well each day and mash the fruit with the hands.

To strain the must from the pulp, it is a good plan to stretch terylene netting or muslin over another bucket, tying it on. Then by standing a colander on two laths over this, the bulk of the fruit is retained in the colander and the liquor enabled to strain through the muslin more easily. Do not squeeze or hurry the process.

Measure the liquid, and to each litre (quart) add 450 g (1 lb) sugar; stir well till dissolved. Leave for four days in a warm place, still covered, then put into fermenting jar and fit an airlock. When fermentation has finished and wine has cleared, rack off into clean bottles and keep six months before using.

171

August

Plum wine (sweet)

Most plums will make a good wine, but generally speaking Victoria plums have been found to be the most satisfactory. Even they sometimes produce a wine which is somewhat lacking in body, and many winemakers, to counter this plum failing, are in the habit of adding a pound of grain (wheat or barley) to the recipe. Plums are rich in pectin, so the use of a pectin-destroying enzyme is essential.

Ingredients	Metric	British	USA
Plums	2.75 kilos	6 lb	5 lb
Sugar	1.5 kilos	3½ lb	2½ lb
Water	4.5 litres	1 gallon	1 gallon
Yeast and nutrient			
Pectic enzyme			

Cut the plums in half, and crush them in your hands. Take half of the water, bring it to the boil, and then pour it over the fruit 'pulp'. Leave it for four or five hours, then add the other half of the water (cold) and the pectic enzyme. Leave for 48 hours, then strain, and you should have about a gallon of really clear juice. Bring this to the boil, and then pour it over the sugar, stirring to dissolve. Allow the liquor to cool to 21°C then add the yeast (preferably a Bordeaux, Tokay or Sauternes yeast or a level teaspoon of granulated yeast), pour the whole into your fermenting vessel, and fit an airlock. When the wine begins to clear, siphon it off for the first time, and when *all* fermentation has finished, rack it again into clean bottles and cork.

Raspberry wine (sweet)

Raspberries have such a strong flavour and aroma that it is difficult to find a niche for them. Both flavour and bouquet are so pronounced that a wine made wholly from them would be unpalatable and have too pronounced a nose. But a dash of raspberry blended into an uninteresting red wine can often bring it to life.

If ever you persuade yourself *not* to eat raspberries, but to make wine with them instead, here is an excellent recipe:

Ingredients	Metric	British	USA
Raspberries	1.75 kilos	4 lb	3 lb
Grape concentrate (red)	300 ml	½ pint	½ pint
Sugar	1.5 kilos	3 lb	2½ lb
Water	4.5 litres	1 gallon	1 gallon
Yeast and nutrient			

Bring the water to the boil and pour it over the fruit, then leave it to cool. Mash the fruit well with the hands, and add pectic enzyme, then cover it closely and leave for four days, stirring daily. Strain through at least two thicknesses of butter muslin on to the sugar and grape concentrate and stir thoroughly to dissolve. Add a good wine yeast (Burgundy, Port or Sauternes is best), or a level teaspoon of granulated yeast, and stir well in. Leave for 24 hours, closely covered, in a warm place, then put the liquor into your fermentation vessel, and fit an airlock. Ferment it right out, and when it clears, siphon the wine off the lees into clean bottles.

Loganberry wine is made in the same way.

* Raspberry and redcurrant wine (sweet)

Ingredients	Metric	British	USA
Raspberries	1.75 kilos	4 lb	3 lb
Redcurrants	1.75 kilos	4 lb	3 lb
Sugar	1.75 kilos	4 lb	3 lb
Water	3.5 litres	About 6 pints	About 6 pints
Yeast and nutrient			

Wash the fruit, rejecting any which are damaged, and press out all the juice. (If a press is not available use a plate and colander stood on laths over a bucket.) Boil the squeezed pulp in three times its own volume of water for two hours, and then strain on to the original juice. The pulp 173

August

should be squeezed dry and this liquid also added. Measure the total liquid thus obtained and to each 4.5 litres (1 gallon) add 1.8 kilos (4 lb) sugar, and then pitch the yeast (when the liquor has cooled to blood heat). Put into fermenting bottle, filling to shoulder to allow space for the vigour of the primary fermentation, but keep a little liquor aside in a covered jug with which to top up once the initial ferment is over. Fit an airlock and leave until fermentation is finished, topping up to bottom of neck as soon as possible. Then siphon off and keep for six months before the final bottling.

Rose petal wine

Many gardens have masses of rose petals which, in the normal course of events, would finish up on the compost heap. But why not take advantage of their glorious scent and make this most unusual wine? All you need is:

Ingredients	Metric	British	USA
Rose petals (the stronger scented the better)	2 litres	2 quarts	2 quarts
Sugar	1.25 kilos	2½ lb	2 lb
Citric acid	2 teaspoons	2 teaspoons	2 teaspoons
Water	4.5 litres	1 gallon	1 gallon
Grape concentrate	280 ml	½ pint	½ pint
Yeast and nutrient			

Bring the water to the boil, and add the sugar, rose petals, the small quantity of grape juice concentrate and juice of the lemon. Stir well, and when it has cooled to 21°C add the yeast (a GP wine yeast or a level teaspoon of granulated yeast and a yeast nutrient). Leave to ferment for a week, stirring daily, and keeping closely covered. Then strain into a fermentation jar and ferment until finished. A wine made in this way will normally have a good colour, if coloured roses are used; if less colour is required the petals should be strained from the liquor three days earlier.

* ## Strawberry wine

Ingredients	Metric	British	USA
Strawberries	2 kilos	4 lb	3 lb
Sugar	1.5 kilos	3 lb	2¼ lb
Citric acid	1 teaspoon	1 teaspoon	1 teaspoon
Grape tannin	½ teaspoon	½ teaspoon	½ teaspoon
Water	4.5 litres	1 gallon	1 gallon
Yeast and nutrient			

Take the stems from the strawberries, and wash the fruit. Mash the berries well, and mix with the sugar and 2 litres (2 quarts) of water. Leave for 24 – 36 hours, then strain liquor into fermenting jar; add a further litre or quart of water to the pulp, mix well, and immediately strain again, then add the acid, tannin, yeast nutrient and yeast, and make up to 4.5 litres (1 gallon) with cold water. Stir thoroughly, fit an airlock, and continue as usual.

* ## Burnet wine (dry)

	Ingredients	Metric	British	USA
	Burnet flowers	2 litres	2 quarts	2 quarts
	Sugar	500 g	1 lb	¾ lb
	Honey	500 g	1 lb	¾ lb
	Raisins	500 g	1 lb	¾ lb
or	Concentrate (red)	280 ml	½ pint	½ pint
	Lemon	1	1	1
	Orange	1	1	1
	Water	4.5 litres	1 gallon	1 gallon
	Yeast and nutrient			

The Greater Salad Burnet, *Sanguisorba officinalis*, is not found much in the south, but is fairly plentiful in the damp meadows of the northern counties, and makes a pleasant light, rosé wine. The plant, however, is rather   175

August

uncooperative, since it opens its blooms in succession up the stem, so that only one zone of flowers is open at the same time. To outwit the plant, pick as many as possible of the flowers as they open, placing them in a bowl of water to infuse. As the other blooms open, they can be added to the first, until half a gallon of blossoms has been picked.

Let these stand for seven days after the last flower has been added, then strain the water on to the sugar, clear honey, and well-chopped raisins or concentrate. Add the juice and a little of the rinds of a lemon and an orange, and simmer for 20 minutes. Cool, then strain into a gallon jar, leaving a little of the liquor for the preparation of a starter. When this is working well, and the must in the jar is lukewarm, stir in the starter, top up the jar with cold water, if necessary, and leave to ferment, closely covered.

Golden rod wine

Method as for Gorse Wine (see April, page 147).

Carrot wine (sweet)

. . . a readily available and very popular drink, with both 'kick' and flavour . . .

Ingredients	Metric	British	USA
Carrots	2.75 kilos	6 lb	5 lb
Wheat	500 g	1 lb	¾ lb
Sugar	1.75 kilos	4 lb	3 lb
Lemons	2	2	2
Oranges	2	2	2
Concentrate	100 ml	4 oz	4 oz
Water	4.5 litres	1 gallon	1 gallon
Yeast and nutrient			

Wash the carrots well but do not peel. Put into the water and bring to the boil; then simmer gently until the carrots are very tender. Use the carrots for food, strain off the water, and make up to one gallon. In a polythene bucket put the sugar, sliced oranges and lemons and pour over them the hot liquid. Stir until the sugar is dissolved, and then stand until lukewarm. Then add the concentrate and wheat and sprinkle the level teaspoonful of granulated yeast on top. Leave to ferment, closely covered, for 15 days, stirring daily. Then skim, strain and put into fermenting jar. Fit an airlock and leave until it is clear and stable. Then bottle. Keep almost a year (from the start of the fermentation) before drinking.

'Folly' or vine prunings wine (medium)

Those of you who are growing vines – and all amateur winemakers should, or they miss a great deal of fun and enjoyment – will have not only grapes (in September) but, throughout the summer, a plentiful supply of vine prunings and leaves as the growing vines are cut back to ensure that the maximum nutrition goes into the bunches of grapes. Do not waste these prunings and leaves; they will make excellent wine! Cut only the green shoots and not ripe wood or the vine will 'bleed'.

The name, incidentally, comes from the French *'feuille'* – leaf!

Ingredients	Metric	British	USA
Leaves and tendrils	2.25 kilos	5 lb	4 lb
Sugar	1.5 kilos	3 lb	2¼ lb
Citric acid	1 teaspoon	1 teaspoon	1 teaspoon
Water	4.5 litres	1 gallon	1 gallon
Yeast and nutrient			

Put the cuttings and leaves into a bowl and pour on to them the boiling water. Let this stand for 48 hours, but turn occasionally to submerge top leaves and keep prunings well under water. Keep bucket closely covered. Pour off liquid and press out remaining leaves and tendrils. 'Wash' the leaves with a pint of water and press again. Dissolve the sugar into the liquid, add the yeast and yeast nutrient, and pour into fermenting vessel and fit an airlock. Ferment right out in the usual way and siphon off when clear.

August

* Pomegranate wine (medium)

Ingredients	Metric	British	USA
Pomegranates	10	10	10
Barley	250 g	½ lb	½ lb
Sugar	1.5 kilos	3 lb	2¼ lb
Citric acid	2 teaspoons	2 teaspoons	2 teaspoons
Water	4.5 litres	1 gallon	1 gallon
Yeast and nutrient			

Clean the outer skins of the pomegranates and meanwhile bring the water to the boil, with the barley in it. Simmer for about five minutes; then strain on to the chopped pomegranates, the sugar, and the citric acid. Stir well. When cool add the nutrient and yeast. Ferment, closely covered, on the pulp for five days, then strain into fermenting jar. Bottle the wine when it clears. An excellent medium table wine.

Ginger beer

If you wish to be popular with the kiddies during the holidays, try making them some ginger beer . . .

Ingredients	Metric	British	USA
Well-bruised root ginger	25 g	1¼ oz	1 oz
Sugar	500 g	1 lb	¾ lb
Lemons	2	2	2
Cream of tartar	¼ teaspoon	¼ teaspoon	¼ teaspoon
Water	4.5 litres	1 gallon	1 gallon
Yeast and nutrient			

Put into a large bowl or polythene bucket the sugar, the rinds (thinly peeled) and the juice of the two lemons, and the well-bruised ginger. Add the squeezed halves of the lemons to the water as it comes to the boil. When it reaches boiling point, pour it over the ingredients in the bucket. Remove lemon halves, stir well and cover. When tepid add the yeast, previously dissolved in a small amount of the warm liquid. Use a small bottle for this, dropping crumbled yeast in and shaking it to dissolve; leave it half-an-hour or more before adding it to the liquor. Lastly, stir in the cream of tartar. Cover and leave for 24 hours. Strain and bottle, and tie down the corks. *Never* use screwstoppers or the bottles may burst. Store in a cool place and drink fairly soon.

Peach perfection (dry)

This is a recipe by the late Mrs Cherry Leeds, of Twickenham, for a peach wine which is so superb – and *cheap* – that we give the fullest possible instructions . . .

It sounds extravagant, but it is not. Keep an eye on the green-grocers and you'll see that in August (usually about the first fortnight) peaches come right down in price, to only a few pence each. The wine works out at about 15p a bottle and in effect one large peach makes one bottle of wine. A Kitzinger sherry or Tokay yeast is best.

To make 10 gallons

Ingredients	Metric	British	USA
Peaches	13.5 kilos	30 lb	25 lb
Sugar, white	10 kilos	22 lb	18 lb
Sugar, brown	4.5 kilos	10 lb	8 lb
Citric acid	75 g	3 oz	3 oz
Grape tannin	1½ teaspoon	1½ teaspoon	1½ teaspoon
Water	45 litres	10 gallons	10 gallons
Yeast and nutrient			
Pectic enzyme			

Wipe peaches and remove the stones; drop into large container such as a polythene bin. Scrub hands well and squeeze the peaches until well mashed. Well cover with boiling water and leave covered overnight.

The next day stir in the pectic enzyme and cover well. On the third day strain through muslin, twice if possible to reduce sludge, and put into the 45 litre (10 gallon) jar; add citric acid, tannin and nutrient.

179

August

At this point it is a simple matter to place the jar or carboy into the position it will occupy during fermentation. Put 9 kilos (20 lb) of sugar into the large container and add sufficient boiling water to dissolve, and when cool add to the jar. Then the level of the liquid is brought up to the turn of the shoulder of the jar with boiled water. Open the yeast bottle, pour in, and re-fit airlock. The gravity at this stage will be about 100; the original gravity is almost invariably 25–30. Fermentation will start on the third day if the temperature is sufficient (21–24°C).

The rest of the sugar is added in stages from now on, the first addition of 2 litres (4 pints) of syrup when the gravity is 30, that is, roughly, after two weeks. The sugar is then added in 1-litre lots when the gravity is between 10 and 15 each time. The syrup used is 1 kilo (2 lb) sugar to 0.5 litre (1 pint) boiling water and cooled, thus making 1 litre syrup.

The fermenting period lasts for about seven or eight months, although you can keep it going for a year with small additions of syrup.

The first racking takes place when all the sugar is in and the reading is 10. Some of the wine will have to be removed to accommodate the last two doses of syrup. Stir up the jar and remove 2 litres (half a gallon). Put it by, under an airlock, and this can be used to top up the jar after the first racking. Stir the liquid vigorously with an oak rod once a day for the first few weeks.

Because of the Pectinol used the wine will clear perfectly and after the first racking will become crystal clear, but don't be tempted to rack it again until fermentation has ceased finally. This usually happens when the gravity is about five.

To make 5 gallons

For the 5-gallon jars use half quantities except the pectic enzyme – this is 2 oz – otherwise the procedure is the same.

To make 4.5 litres (1 gallon)

Ingredients	Metric	British	USA
Peaches	1.5 kilos	3 lb	2¼ lb
Sugar	1.5 kilos	3 lb	2¼ lb
Citric acid	1 teaspoon	1 teaspoon	1 teaspoon
Grape tannin	½ teaspoon	½ teaspoon	½ teaspoon

Boiling water	4.5 litres	1 gallon	1 gallon
Yeast made up as a 1-pint starter.			
Yeast nutrient		2 oz	
Pectic enzyme		2 oz	

The method is the same but the yeast starter bottle is prepared on the same day as mashing, and the sugar is put in all together, just before the yeast starter.

Apricot wine As Peach

Pea-pod wine (medium)

Despite its somewhat unattractive and prosaic name (a chance here for someone to invent a better one!), this is a light attractive wine which is a great favourite with many winemakers. Certainly no one can complain that the ingredients are expensive!

Ingredients	Metric	British	USA
Pea pods	2.25 kilos	5 lb	4 lb
Sugar	1.5 kilos	3 lb	2 ¼ lb
Citric acid	1 tablespoon	1 tablespoon	1 tablespoon
Grape tannin	½ teaspoon	½ teaspoon	½ teaspoon
Water	4.5 litres	1 gallon	1 gallon
Yeast and nutrient			

Wash the pods carefully, and then boil them in the water until they are tender, then strain and dissolve the sugar in the warm liquid. Add the yeast, and other ingredients, pour into jar, and fit an airlock. Siphon off when wine begins to clear and bottle when fermentation has ceased.

181

August

* Greengage wine (sweet)

Ingredients	Metric	British	USA
Plums or greengages	1.75 kilos	4 lb	3 lb
Barley	0.25 kilo	½ lb	½ lb
Sugar	1.75 kilos	4 lb	3 lb
Water	4.5 litres	1 gallon	1 gallon
Yeast and nutrient			
Pectic enzyme			

Grind the barley in the mincer, stone and cut up the fruit, putting both into a bin. Pour over them boiling water, cover closely and leave for four days, adding the pectic enzyme when cool. The enzyme is most important if you are to be sure of a haze-free wine. Stir daily. Then strain on to the sugar, add the yeast nutrient and stir till all is dissolved. Then add the yeast (preferably a Burgundy wine yeast, but failing that a general-purpose wine yeast or a level teaspoonful of granulated yeast). Keep closely covered in a warm place for a week, then pour into fermenting jar, filling to bottom of neck, and fit an airlock. Siphon off for the first time when it clears but do not bottle until assured that fermentation has completely finished.

Bullace, damson and plum wines

Method and quantities as for Greengage.

* Red gooseberry (dry)

Ingredients	Metric	British	USA
Red gooseberries	1.75 kilos	4 lb	3 lb
Sugar	1.5 kilos	3 lb	2¼ lb
Water	4.5 litres	1 gallon	1 gallon
Yeast and nutrient			
Pectic enzyme			

September

Pick the ripe gooseberries on a dry day, choosing large and juicy fruits. Top and tail and mash well in a bowl before adding the enzyme and yeast. Pour on the cold water and allow to stand three days, stirring twice a day. Strain well through nylon net and dissolve the sugar in the juice. Then put into fermenting jar and fit trap and leave until wine has cleared and fermented out. Then siphon off into clean bottles and cork.

Elderberry and runner bean wine

This sounds a most unlikely combination, to be sure, but the fact is that it makes a first-class and well-balanced wine. I was first introduced to it many years ago by that well-known winemaker, Mr S. W. Andrews, and find that the runner beans do mitigate the harshness of straight elderberry, so it pays to put a few pounds into your deep freeze each year to be sure of having some when the elderberries are ready. Gardeners should not have that difficulty!

Ingredients	Metric	British	USA
Elderberries	1 kilo	2½ lb	2 lb
Red grape concentrate	200 ml	8 oz	6 oz
Runner beans	450 g	1 lb	¾ lb
Sugar	1.3 g	3 lb	2½ lb
Tartaric acid	7 g	1½ teaspoons	1 teaspoon
Vitamin B_1 tablet	1	1	1
Yeast and nutrient			
Water	4.5 litres	1 gallon	1 gallon

Boil up some fresh, young runner beans in a little of the water; do not use the water in which beans have been cooked for the table, since it will have been salted. Strain off the bean liquor. Put the elderberries into a plastic bucket and pour over them the rest of the water, boiling. Add the sugar and stir well, and pulp the elderberries with a kitchen spoon or potato masher, then add the bean liquor.

When cool add the acid, vitamin tablet, nutrient and yeast. Cover closely, and ferment on the pulp for four days, stirring daily. Then strain into a fermenting jar and fit an airlock. The wine will ferment out quickly

September

but will be longer than most in maturing, even with the help of the runner beans. If you need to speed the process, the cautious addition of a little glycerine is recommended, and you may well find that one of the modern artificial maturing agents now on sale in wine shops is a help.

Passion fruit wine (dry)

And this doesn't mean what you're thinking! The passion fruit, or purple granadilla, is of the Passifloraceae. The passiflora, or passion flower, is so called because its several parts symbolise the story of the Passion of Our Lord. Two types produce edible fruit – *P. edulis* and *P. quadrangularis*, rather like plums. The ordinary garden passion flower (*P. caerulea*) does not.

Ingredients	Metric	British	USA
Passion fruit	2 kilos	4 lb	3 lb
Barley	250 g	½ lb	½ lb
Sugar	1 kilo	2½ lb	2 lb
Water	4.5 litres	1 gallon	1 gallon
Yeast and nutrient			
Pectic enzyme			

As for Plum Wine, but the fruit will need to be grated.

Apple wine (1) (medium)

This is a truly delicious wine, and although apparently heavy on fruit is well worth making. It is strong, yet delicately flavoured, with an attractive, faintly 'cidery' bouquet.

Ingredients	Metric	British	USA
Apples (mixed windfalls)	10 kilos	24 lb	18 lb
Sugar (to the gallon of liquor)	1.5 kilos	3 lb	2¼ lb
Yeast and nutrient			
Water	4.5 litres	1 gallon	1 gallon

Chop the apples into small pieces, put into a bin, add the yeast and water (the water will not cover the apples). Leave for about a week, stirring vigorously several times a day to bring the apples at the bottom to the top. Keep the bin closely covered and in a fairly warm place. Then strain the juice from the apple 'pulp'. Press the juice from the apples and add to the rest of the liquor. To every 4.5 litres (1 gallon) add 1.5 kilos (3 lb) of sugar. Put into fermenting vessel and fit an airlock, racking when it has cleared. The wine will be ready for drinking within six months, but improves for being kept a year.

If eating apples are used it is a good idea to make every tenth pound one of crab apples, and another improvement is to employ a Sauternes wine yeast.

* Apple wine (2) (dry)

Ingredients	Metric	British	USA
Apples	2.75 kilos	6 lb	5 lb
Sugar	1 kilo	2½ lb	2¼ lb
Concentrate (white)	150 ml	¼ pint	¼ pint
Citric acid	1 teaspoon	1 teaspoon	1 teaspoon
Water	4.5 litres	1 gallon	1 gallon
Yeast and nutrient			

Wash and cut up the apples, skins, brown patches and all. Windfalls will do. Simmer 10–15 minutes in one gallon of water. Strain liquid on to the sugar, and the thinly peeled rind of the lemon. Stir well. When lukewarm add the juice of the lemon, the yeast and the yeast nutrient to the liquid, and the concentrate, cover and leave for 24 hours in a warm place, then pour into a fermenting jar, cover with three layers of clean nylon material, or insert an airlock. Leave in a warm place to ferment for four weeks. Siphon off into clean dry storage jar, and ferment out under airlock. Then siphon off and mature for six months before bottling.

September

* Elderberry wine (sweet)

Ingredients	Metric	British	USA
Elderberries	1.5 kilos	3 lb	2¼ lb
Sugar	1.5 kilos	3½ lb	2½ lb
Citric acid	1 teaspoon	1 teaspoon	1 teaspoon
Water	4.5 litres	1 gallon	1 gallon
Yeast and nutrient			

Strip the berries from the stalks by using the prongs of an ordinary table fork (otherwise it is a messy and tedious business), then weigh them and crush them in a bowl. Pour on the boiling water, and let it cool to about 21°C before adding yeast and acid. Leave three days, stirring daily, then strain through fine sieve on to the sugar. Pour the liquid into a dark glass bottle (in clear bottles the wine may lose its colour), but do not fill completely until first vigorous ferment has subsided, plugging the neck with cottonwool. When the ferment is quieter fill to the bottom of neck, and fit an airlock. Leave until fermentation is complete – it may be longer than most – then siphon off into clean, dark bottles and keep for six months at least.

Mead (dry or sweet)
(by S. H. Pullinger, Alresford)

Take 1.5–2 kilos (3–4½ lb) of mild honey, amount according to dryness or sweetness of wine required. If a wine yeast is to be used, have it activated and ready in advance.

Bring the honey to the boil in two or three times its volume of water. Stir with stainless steel spoon until honey is dissolved, or it may burn. Skim off any scum which rises.

To the hot liquid add approximately 15 g (½ oz) of citric acid and the yeast nutrient. Alternatively, you may use the juice of 4–6 lemons, when only half the yeast nutrient need be added.

Add the rest of the water when convenient, transfer to fermenting container and add yeast when cool. A narrow neck and airlock are advisable. Since there are 4.5 litres (1 gallon) of water and 2 kilos of honey

September

there will be about 4 to 5 litres (9 to 10 pints) of liquid. This will allow for a full gallon (4.5 litres) after racking, which should take place when the wine is beginning to clear and a definite layer of sludge can be seen at the bottom. Wine made now would be worth drinking at Christmas but would be better for keeping.

Sweet melomel (rosehip mead)

If you wish to use rosehips for flavouring to make *Melomel,* as a fruit flavoured mead is called, use about 4 lb. Boil them in a gallon of water for 5 or 10 minutes, and when cool mash them with your hands or a piece of hardwood, and strain through butter muslin.

To this add 4 lb of honey, 15 g citric acid and yeast nutrient, and stir until the honey is dissolved. When lukewarm add the yeast and ferment as usual. It is an improvement for this mead to use a sherry yeast and ferment in the sherry manner, i.e. *after the first racking* (not before) have your fermenting container only ⅞ full, and use an empty airlock, the end of which can be lightly plugged with a small piece of cotton wool, thus exposing the mead to air but preventing the entrance of any vinegar flies, allowing a degree of oxidisation. But you can also use an ordinary wine yeast and ferment and mature throughout in the usual way if you wish.

Metheglin

To make *Metheglin* use 4 lb honey, 1 oz hops, and 15 g (½ oz) root ginger to the gallon, or with the same amount of honey and water, 2 cloves and 10 g (¼ oz) cinnamon bark, or 5 g (⅛ oz) or caraway seeds.

Marjoram, balm, mace, lemon and orange peel, and cinnamon, are also flavourings which can be tried, but it is as well not to overdo them. 187

September

* Sparkling mead

Ingredients	Metric	British	USA
Honey	1.5 kilos	3 lb	2¼ lb
Citric acid	1 tablespoon	1 tablespoon	1 tablespoon
Water	4.5 litres	1 gallon	1 gallon
Maury or wine yeast and nutrient			

Bring the water to the boil for a minute or so, and then allow it to cool to 50°C. Warm up the honey meantime to the same temperature, and then mix the two, stirring well to dissolve the honey.

Allow the honey liquor to cool to 21°C and then add the acid, a good yeast nutrient and the prepared yeast culture. Failing this, you can use a level teaspoonful of granulated yeast, but there is then a risk, if racking should happen to be delayed later on, of spoiling the delicate mead flavour. Pour the liquid into a fermenting jar, filling it to the shoulder of the jar, and keep the surplus in a separate airlocked bottle nearby. Put both vessels in a warm place (17–21°C). If the fermentation froths out of the jar, as it may do, top up from the bottle. When the vigorous ferment slows down, and froth ceases to form, fill the jar to the bottom of the neck, fit an airlock, and clean the exterior if necessary. When fermentation stops completely move the jar to a cold room and leave it there for a fortnight or three weeks before siphoning the mead off the lees, and into a clean jar. Use a well-fitting close-grained cork, driven well home, but do not wire it down. The following March (after roughly six months' storage) siphon the mead off the lees again and to the gallon add 50 g (2 oz) honey (or white sugar) dissolved in 150 ml (¼ pint) of water, boiled and cooled as before. Mix thoroughly and bottle, using strong bottles (of champagne type, if possible), cork, and wire or tie the corks down.

Note that honey is usually deficient in trace minerals and is sometimes difficult to ferment. It is therefore important to use a yeast nutrient.

* Blackberry wine (medium)

Ingredients	Metric	British	USA
Blackberries	1.75 kilos	4 lb	3 lb
Sugar	1.5 kilos	3 lb	2¼ lb
Water	4.5 litres	1 gallon	1 gallon
Yeast nutrient			
Pectic enzyme			

The fruit should be picked when ripe and dry, on a sunny day. Wash it well, being careful to remove any of the small maggots sometimes found in blackberries. Place the fruit in a polythene bucket, and crush it with a potato masher. Pour over it the boiling water. Stir well, allow to become lukewarm (about 21°C), then add the pectic enzyme according to instructions, and a day later the yeast and nutrient. Cover closely and leave for four or five days, stirring daily. Strain through some nylon netting or a nylon sieve on to 1.5 kilos (3 lb) of granulated sugar. Stir well to make sure that all is dissolved. Pour into dark fermenting jar, filling to shoulder, and fit an airlock. Keep the spare liquor in a smaller bottle also fitted with a trap or plug of cotton wool. When the ferment quietens sufficiently for there to be no risk of it foaming through the trap (after, say, a week) top up with the spare wine to the base of the neck and refit trap. Leave until it clears and then rack for the first time.

Dewberry, loganberry and raspberry wines

... can be made to exactly the same recipe as Blackberry Wine.

189

September

* Medlar wine

Ingredients	Metric	British	USA
Medlars	2.75 kilos	6 lb	5 lb
Sugar	1.5 kilos	3 lb	2¼ lb
Grape tannin	½ teaspoon	½ teaspoon	½ teaspoon
Water	4.5 litres	1 gallon	1 gallon
Yeast and nutrient			
Pectic enzyme			

Chop the fruit and pour over it 2 litres (quarts) boiling water; stir in half the sugar, and 1 quart cold water. Leave till cool, then add remaining ingredients. Cover closely and leave in warm place. After three days strain into fermenting jar and top up to bottom of neck with cold water. Fit an airlock and continue as usual.

* Blackberry and apple (sweet)

Ingredients	Metric	British	USA
Blackberries	900 g	2 lb	2 lb
Apples	3.5 kilos	8 lb	6 lb
Concentrated grape juice	150 ml	¼ pint	¼ pint
Pectolase	5 g	1 teaspoon	1 teaspoon
Vitamin B_1 tablet	1	1	1
Sugar	1 kilo	2½ lb	2 lb
Water to	4.5 litres	1 gallon	1 gallon
Yeast and nutrient			

If you have an extractor express the juice from the apples, otherwise liquidise them or crush them after chopping them. Put the juice or pulp to one side and put the washed blackberries into a polythene bucket. Put the sugar into a saucepan and just cover it with some of the water; bring it to the boil until the syrup clarifies. Pour the boiling syrup over the fruit, stir well, and then add the apple juice or pulp. Allow to cool, and then add

3 pints of water, the vitamin tablet, concentrate, pectolase, yeast and nutrient. Ferment on the pulp for five days, once the fermentation has got going, then strain into a fermenting jar. If the ferment is not too vigorous top up with cold water to the bottom of the neck and fit an airlock. Ferment out, rack and bottle in the usual way.

Cider or perry

Cider is made from apples, perry from pears.

Strictly speaking, only natural sugar of the fruit should be employed and no sugar should be added.

A press or juice extractor is essential. Put the fruit in a tub or polythene dustbin and crush it with a 'masher', a heavy baulk of timber. Then express the juice by means of a press or by wrapping the fruit a little at a time in a stout cloth and twisting or pressing it. Collect the juice in a jar, stand it on a tray in a warm place (about 21°C) and add yeast. Invert a small glass over the top of the jar. For a few days the jar will froth over and must be kept topped up, but when the ferment quietens fit an airlock and proceed as for any other wine.

* Pear wine (dry)

Ingredients	Metric	British	USA
Pears	2.25 kilos	5 lb	4 lb
Sugar	1 kilo	2½ lb	2 lb
Citric acid	1 teaspoon	1 teaspoon	1 teaspoon
Water	4.5 litres	1 gallon	1 gallon
Yeast and nutrient			

Really ripe pears, even 'sleepy' ones, are best for your purpose. Do not bother to peel or core them, but chop them, being careful to save any juice, put them into a large saucepan, and add the water and any juice. Bring slowly to the boil, and simmer gently for not more than 20 minutes, or the wine may not clear later. Strain the liquor on to the sugar in a fermenting bin and add the acid and yeast nutrient, since pears are deficient in both.

191

September

When the liquor has cooled to blood heat transfer to a fermenting jar, add a wine yeast or a level teaspoonful of granulated yeast, and fit an airlock.

Do not fill the jar to the bottom of the neck but keep a little of the liquor aside in another airlocked bottle, to be added when the first vigorous fermentation has quietened and there is no longer risk of the wine foaming out through the airlock. An excellent wine can be made in this way, but if you have a fondness for really dry wine, for which pears are particularly suitable, cut the sugar down until the original gravity of the liquor is about 1090, or 1 kilo per 4.5 litres (2 lb 3 oz per gallon).

* Mulberry wine (dry)

Ingredients	Metric	British	USA
Mulberries	1.5 kilos	3½ lb	2½ lb
Concentrate (red)	280 ml	½ pint	½ pint
Sugar	1 kilo	2 lb	1½ lb
Campden tablet	1	1	1
Water	4.5 litres	1 gallon	1 gallon
Yeast and nutrient			
Pectic enzyme			

Wash the mulberries, having removed the stalks, and put them and the concentrate into your polythene bucket. Pour on the boiling water; when cool add the crushed Campden tablet, the pectic enzyme, half the sugar, the nutrient, and the yeast. Stir well. Ferment for four days on pulp, then strain into fermenting jar, add remaining sugar, and ferment, rack and bottle in the usual way. A Bordeaux yeast is preferable.

* Rosehip wine (medium)

Ingredients	Metric	British	USA
Fresh rosehips	1 kilo	2 lb	2 lb
or Dried rosehips	250 g	½ lb	½ lb

Citric acid	1 teaspoon	1 teaspoon	1 teaspoon
Sugar	1.5 kilos	3 lb	2¼ lb
Water	4.5 litres	1 gallon	1 gallon
Yeast and nutrient			
Pectic enzyme			

The best time to gather your rosehips, of which there are usually plenty in the hedgerows, is immediately after the first frost. Wash them well, and then cut them in half or crush them with a piece of wood or mallet. (This is unnecessary with the dried rosehips.) Put the sugar into a polythene bucket, with the crushed rosehips, and pour over them the boiling water. Stir well to dissolve the sugar. When the liquor has cooled sufficiently for you to be able to put your finger in it comfortably, add yeast (a general purpose wine yeast, or a level teaspoon of granulated yeast), acid, enzyme, and nutrient. Leave in a warm place, cover closely for a fortnight, and stir daily. Then strain through a sieve, or some nylon netting, into a fermentation jar and fit an airlock. When the wine clears (after about three months) siphon into a fresh jar, and leave for a further three months before racking again and bottling. Since the only main ingredient which has to be bought is the sugar, this is a most economical wine to make, and I am told that the hips contain a high proportion of Vitamin C, so it is probably beneficial as well!

Rosehips store well in a domestic freezer. Coarsely mince them and freeze them in bags containing 2 lb each. Each bag has then the correct amount of rosehips to make a gallon of wine. These make a delightful social wine, if 6 oz of chopped dried figs are included in the recipe, and the eventual wine is sweetened to taste.

Rosehip syrup, as produced for infants, was a popular ingredient for winemaking. However, this product is no longer available. It is possible to make your own from fresh rosehips.

As well as dried rosehips, your local homebrew shop may be able to supply rosehip shells. These are dried rosehips minus the seeds. Use them at three-quarters the rate quoted in recipes for dried rosehips, e.g. 8 oz dried rosehips = 6 oz rosehip shells.

September

* Rowanberry wine (medium)

Ingredients	Metric	British	USA
Rowanberries	1.5 kilos	3 lb	2¼ lb
Concentrate (red)	280 ml	½ pint	½ pint
Wheat	250 g	½ lb	½ lb
Sugar	1.25 kilos	3 lb	2½ lb
Water	4.5 litres	1 gallon	1 gallon
Citric acid	1 tablespoon	1 tablespoon	1 tablespoon
Yeast and nutrient			

Pour the boiling water over the berries and let it stand for four days, then strain. Put in the sugar, concentrate, acid, and wheat and stir until the sugar is dissolved, then add the yeast and nutrient. Leave to ferment 16 days, closely covered, then strain into fermenting jar and fit an airlock. When it clears, siphon into bottles, corking lightly at first.

* Red table wine

Ingredients	Metric	British	USA
Elderberries	4.5 kilos	10 lb	8 lb
Concentrate (red)	2.5 litres	5 pints	5 pints
Sugar	2 kilos	4 lb	3 lb
Water	18 litres	4½ gallons	4½ gallons
Beaujolais yeast and nutrient			

Crush the elderberries and strain off the juice. Leach the pulp by adding 4.5 litres (1 gallon) of boiling water, stirring for five minutes and then straining off the liquid. Press lightly. Repeat this treatment with a similar quantity of boiling water. Add the concentrate, and nutrients to this elderberry extract, followed by another 7 litres (1½ gallons) of water. When cool add the yeast starter and ferment for four days. Add the sugar, stir until completely dissolved, and make up the volume to 18 litres (4½ gallons) with water. Thereafter continue as usual with fermenting, racking and bottling.

Grape wine

Many people who have a vine, or a few vines, are puzzled as to how to convert their grapes into wine, but in essentials nothing could be simpler.

First, make sure that your grapes are as ripe as possible (the birds will tell you when they are nearly ready, if the vine is unprotected!), gather them, and set to work quickly. All you have to do is to ferment the grape juice, but it is as well to note that, if making small quantities, with a consequent high degree of wastage, as much as between 6 and 7 kilos (12 and 15 lb) of grapes will be required to produce 4.5 litres (1 gallon) of wine. About 2 kilos (4 lb) will make one bottle. And, even in one of our sunniest summers, when the sugar content of our grapes will perhaps be higher than usual, it is likely that you must expect to have to add some sugar, if a reasonably strong wine is required. If you use a hydrometer, it is simple to ascertain how much, but if you do not, no matter; the solution then is to aim at a strong wine, say 12 – 14 per cent of alcohol by volume,

The author showing Evelyn Barrett some of the 1995 crop of Seyval grapes.

195

September

and to continue adding the sugar in small quantities of, say 100 g to 4.5 litres (4 oz to the gallon) at a time, until the ferment is carried as far as it will go, and the sweetness of the wine is to your taste.

Many beginners seem to be puzzled by the difference between white wine and red, and ask whether black grapes can be employed to produce the former. The answer is: yes. White wine can be made from grapes of either colour (although it should be noted that there are some black grapes, e.g. Baco No. 1, which give red juice), the method being to express the juice and ferment it alone. Red wine on the other hand is produced by leaving the skins of the crushed black grapes in the must, so that the colour from them is extracted.

If the skins are left in only one or two days a vin rosé will be produced, if longer a wine of much deeper colour. This process can usually be continued for about 10 days, but it is unwise to leave it much longer, and the liquid should then be drawn off.

A press, of course, is invaluable, and essential if making large quantities of white wine, but most winemakers will be able to contrive to

Fresh-picked grapes, Seyval and Baco No. 1, ready for the press.

press enough grapes for one or two gallons without one, by crushing with the hands or a piece of hard wood, or by using boards and weights, or some similar device. For white wine, of course, the grapes must be contained in stout calico or some such material to keep the skins separate.

Aim at a strength of 12–14 per cent alcohol by volume. If using a hydrometer, express the juice from a few of the grapes and measure the SG. With English grapes it is likely to be fairly low, about 50 or 60, and to obtain the desired strength you will need to add 15–20 oz of sugar. It may be higher, if so, consult the table on page 199, given by E. Chancrin in *Le Vin*.

(If you have no hydrometer, make a mental note of the fact that you are likely to have to add *up to* 1 kilo (2 lb) of sugar to each 4.5 litres (1 gallon), but do it by stages, adding 250 g (8 oz) initially and thereafter 100 g (4 oz) at a time.)

If you are making wine from grapes for the first time it is unlikely that you will want to bother your head unduly about acidity, for *if the grapes are really ripe* any slight over-acidity can be masked by a little extra sugar once the wine is made. But for the perfectionist it is as well to note that grapes – and certainly English grapes – are likely to be slightly too acid, and probably contain about 1.30 per cent acid, whereas the desirable acidity is about 0.75 per cent. The experienced winemaker will go to the trouble of correcting this by diluting with water or syrup, but for the present purpose this is an unnecessary complication. In practice with my red Baco No. 1 grapes I find it is invariably necessary to add as much as a quarter of the volume of grape juice in water to obtain a reasonable acidity. Do this before taking the hydrometer reading. Aim at the acidity of a good cooking apple.

This is usually so with red grapes, which are more difficult to ripen and therefore achieve a reasonably low acidity. My own practice, after diluting to get the acidity right, is to restore the vinosity by the addition of some red grape concentrate, usually at the rate of 150–200 ml to 5 litres. This restores the strength of flavour and improves the rather poor flavour of my Baco No. 1 grapes.

The SG is then taken and sugar added as necessary, to give a reading of 1085–1090, to produce a dry red wine.

The white grapes are usually much riper and need but very little acid adjustment, although some chaptalisation (sugar addition) is generally necessary.

Seyval vine growing on the wall of the author's house.

September

In recent years I have tackled the problem of acidity both when making up the must and by adjusting the finished clear wine in the one-gallon jar just before bottling. Generally I find it necessary to use either an acid-reducing solution, if the over-acidity is slight, or the addition of more water until it is correct. An inclusion of one, or even two, drops of Sweetex, a tablet or teaspoon of Apartame (Canderel), or some other form of non-fermenting sweetener per bottle gives me a most acceptable result with this particular white grape, the Seyval. But whatever variety you have, it is always worth experimenting with the *finished* wine to bring it up to top standard. The same is true, of course, of all other country wines. Never be content to drink a sub-standard wine, just because "but that's how it turned out", if by minor adjustments to strength, sweetness, acidity, or even flavour, you can make an improvement. Always experiment with a small *measured* sample, so that you can calculate the dosages needed for the whole batch.

SG of grape juice	Approx. number of ounces of sugar to be added to one gallon to increase alcohol (by volume) to:		
	10%	14%	18%
1050	11	20	32
1055	9	17	29
1060	7	15	27
1065	5	13	25
1070	3	11	23
1075	—	10	21
1080	—	8	20
1085	—	6	18
1090	—	4	16
1095	—	2	14
1100	—	—	12
1105	—	—	10
1110	—	—	8
1115	—	—	6
1120	—	—	4
1125	—	—	2
1130	—	—	—

October

White wine

Discard any mouldy or unsound grapes, remove the stems, and break the skins of the grapes by crushing or pounding them, then express the juice by means of a press or by crushing with the hands, the fruit being in a calico or sacking bag. If using a press, apply pressure gradually; it is better to repeat the pressing once or twice slowly, than to try to force it for if your press is a small one you may strain it and, what is worse, squirt pulp and juice all over the walls! Let the juice run freely and only apply pressure again when the flow has dropped back to a dribble.

If using a hydrometer, test the juice and determine how much sugar has to be added; dissolve it in the juice, and pour the juice into your fermenting vessel. (Many winemakers prefer to add only half the sugar at this stage and the remainder two or three days later.)

You can either (a) rely upon the natural yeast (the bloom upon the grapes, of which sufficient will have passed into the juice to start fermentation) or, preferably (b) add one Campden tablet per gallon, and, 24 hours later, a vigorous yeast starter of your own choice. A good yeast nutrient will also help.

Fermentation, in a warm place, will be more rapid than with the usual run of country wines, but the advent of chillier weather will slow it down.

If you are not using a hydrometer, of course, add your initial 250 g (8 oz) of sugar, and therefore keep a close eye on your ferment, for it is likely to require further sugar almost every day, although the ferment and sugar consumption will be slower in the later stages than in the early one.

Thereafter the process is the same as with any country wine.

Red wine

If using a hydrometer, press a few of the grapes to determine the specific gravity of the juice and how much sugar to add. If not using a hydrometer, it is best to add at least 500 g (1 ¼ lb).

Remove the stalks of the grapes: place the grapes in a tub or bin and crush them by hand or with a piece of hardwood and, if using the natural yeast, add the sugar and yeast nutrient, stirring very thoroughly. If using a specific yeast add one Campden tablet per gallon, and 24 hours

Grapes in the 'scratcher', or crusher . . .   . . . and being pressed.

later stir in the sugar and add the yeast.

Use a disc of heavy hardwood (oak or beech), fitting very loosely in the cylindrical bin, to hold the skins down below the surface of the liquid. Bore holes in it with a 2 in bit. Each day push this 'sinker' down to keep the skins wet. This is important or you may get poor colour extraction and the 'cap' of skins may acetify. Keep the bin in a warm place for up to 10 days, according to the depth of colour you require, but no more, then strain off the liquor into your fermenting vessel and add (by stages if not using a hydrometer) the balance of the sugar. If you can, press the pulp to get 'just that little extra'.

Keep this wine, of course, in an opaque or coloured fermenter to preserve its colour, and therefore continue as for any ordinary country wine.

October

* Hawthornberry wine (dry)

Ingredients	Metric	British	USA
Hawthornberries	2.25 litres	½ gallon	½ gallon
White grape juice concentrate	280 ml	½ pint	½ pint
Sugar	1.25 kilos	2½ lb	2 lb
Pectolase	5 ml	1 teaspoon	1 teaspoon
Citric acid	15 g	1 tablespoon	2 tablespoons
Water	4.5 litres	1 gallon	1 gallon
Campden tablet	1	1	1
Yeast and nutrient			

Rinse the berries to remove dust and 'foreign bodies' and pour over them six pints of boiling water. Leave to cool, then crush them with a stainless steel spoon (or your hands) and stir in the pectolase, crushed Campden tablet, and acid. Twenty-four hours later add the concentrated grape juice, sugar, yeast and nutrient. Keep covered in a warm place for five days, then strain into a one-gallon jar, top up with water to base of neck, fit trap, and continue as usual.

* Bilberry wine (medium)

Ingredients	Metric	British	USA
Fresh bilberries	1.5 kilos	3 lb	3 lb
Sugar	1.5 kilos	3 lb	2¼ lb
Citric acid	2 teaspoons	1 dessertspoon	1 tablespoon
Water	4.5 litres	1 gallon	1 gallon
Yeast and nutrient			

Pour half the water, boiling, over the bilberries, and stir in the sugar, and, when the liquor has cooled, add the remaining water (cold), the acid, nutrient and yeast. Cover and ferment on the pulp for four or five days before straining into a jar and fitting an airlock. Thereafter proceed as usual.

Cranberry wine

... can be made to the same recipe.

* Sloe wine

	Ingredients	Metric	British	USA
	Sloes	1.5 kilos	3 lb	2¼ lb
	Raisins	0.25 kilo	½ lb	½ lb
or	Concentrate (red)	140 ml	¼ pint	¼ pint
	Sugar	1.5 kilos	3 lb	2½ lb
	Water	3.5 litres	6 pints	6 pints
	Yeast and nutrient			
	Pectic enzyme			

Place the sloes in a bucket or bowl and pour over them the boiling water. Mash the sloes well, adding the minced raisins or concentrate, and, when cool, the pectic enzyme, followed 24 hours later by the yeast and nutrient, 2lb sugar and, of course, the yeast. Stir well, cover with a cloth and ferment in a warm room for 10 days, stirring each day. Then strain, add remaining sugar, and pour into fermenting jar, topping up to bottom of neck with cold water. Fit an airlock and leave in a warm room for four weeks to ferment, then taste. If too bitter, a little more sugar can be added. Refit an airlock and store in a cool place to clear for a few weeks. When clear, bottle and store for at least a year before use.

Sloe gin

Half-fill a 1-kilo clean preserving glass jar with a screw-on lid with pricked clean sloes, adding 125 g (4 oz) of caster sugar, and fill the jar up to the top with dry gin.

Place the sealing ring on the top, and screw the lid down tightly. Shake the jar daily until the sugar is dissolved and the liquid has taken on

November

a dark colour. 10 ml (¼ oz) of almond essence can be added after two weeks.

Leave the sloes in the jar for two months in all, shaking up fairly often. When the gin is to be bottled, preferably in a half-size liqueur bottle, the liquid must be run through linen or a filter to ensure all particles which would otherwise mar the clarity are kept from the bottle.

* English port

Ingredients	Metric	British	USA
Elderberries	900 g	2 lb	1¾ lb
Blackberries	900 g	2 lb	1¾ lb
Sloes	450 g	1 lb	¾ lb
Blackcurrants	450 g	1 lb	¾ lb
Red grape concentrate	150 ml	¼ pint	¼ pint
Sugar	1.3 g	3 lb	2½ lb
Vitamin B₁ tablet	1	1	1
Pectolase	10 g	2 teaspoons	1 teaspoon
Port yeast and nutrient			
Water to	4.5 litres	1 gallon	1 gallon

A mixture of fruits like this often produces some of the best wines, and the making of such wines, in which the fruits do not all ripen at the same time, is greatly simplified now that most households have a freezer and can keep fruit indefinitely. Just cover the sugar with some of the water and bring it to the boil, then pour it over the crushed fruit, in a polythene bucket. When it cools, stir in the grape concentrate and pectolase, and next day the vitamin B_1, yeast, nutrient, and 5 pints water.

Ferment on the pulp for at least five days, then strain into fermenting jar and make up to 1 gallon. Ferment out, rack, and bottle as usual.

* Sugar beet wine (dry)

Ingredients	Metric	British	USA
Sugar beet	2 kilos	4½ lb	3 lb
Sugar	1 kilo	2 lb 2 oz	1½ lb
Bruised ginger	25 g	1 oz	1 oz
Water	4.5 litres	9 pints	9 pints
Yeast and nutrient			

This is a recipe which makes a sturdy, dry wine of 15.4 per cent alcohol by volume.

Wash or scrub the beet, slice them and boil with the ginger in 3 litres (7 pints) of the water for 1½ hours. Then strain on to the remaining cold water. If you wish you can press the beet (as I did) thus obtaining an extra half-pint of liquor. To this add 1 kilo (2 lb 2 oz) of sugar and boil in for three-quarters of an hour. Make up to 4.5 litres (1 gallon) if necessary, allow to cool until tepid, then pour into fermenting jar, add yeast and nutrient, and fit an airlock. Leave for three months, then siphon into fresh jars or bottles. A warming wine for winter nights!

* Apricot wine (medium)

Ingredients	Metric	British	USA
Dried apricots	1 kilo	2 lb	1½ lb
Wheat	500 g	1 lb	¾ lb
Sugar	1.5 kilos	3 lb	2¼ lb
Citric acid	2 teaspoons	2 teaspoons	2 teaspoons
Grape tannin	1 teaspoon	1 teaspoon	1 teaspoon
Water	4.5 litres	1 gallon	1 gallon
Yeast and nutrient			
Pectic enzyme			

205

November

Cut up the apricots, put into 4.5 litres (1 gallon) of water, and bring to the boil; simmer for half-an-hour, then strain (without pressing). Add the other ingredients to the liquor and, when cool enough, the yeast, and enzyme; ferment for three weeks, closely covered, in a warm place, stir daily. Strain into a fermenting bottle, make up with cold water to 4.5 litres, fit an airlock, and ferment for a further month. Then strain, bottle, and cork tightly.

* Celery wine (medium)

Ingredients	Metric	British	USA
Celery (green and white)	2 kilos	4 lb	3 lb
Sugar	1.5 kilos	3 lb	2¼ lb
Citric acid	1 tablesp.	1 tablesp.	1 tablesp.
Water	4.5 litres	1 gallon	1 gallon
Yeast and nutrient			

Chop up the celery into short lengths and boil it in the water until it is tender to extract the flavour. Strain (if you like you can use the cooked celery as a vegetable) and stir in sugar and acid. If you require wine of a golden colour use Demerara instead of white. Then, when you are sure all the sugar has dissolved, allow the liquor to cool to 21°C before adding the yeast (a GP wine yeast or a level teaspoon of granulated yeast) and yeast nutrient. Keep in a bucket or bowl, closely covered, in a warm place for four days, then stir well, transfer to fermenting jar, fit an airlock. Leave until it clears, then siphon off the lees. Leave until fermentation has completely finished, there is a firm sediment, and wine is really clear, before siphoning into clean bottles as usual. The slight bitterness of this wine makes it an excellent aperitif.

* Clove and ginger wine

Ingredients	Metric	British	USA
Cloves	30 g	1 oz	1 oz

November

Light brown sugar	1.5 kilos	3 lb	2¼ lb
Ginger	30 g	1 oz	1 oz
Lemons	3	3	3
Seville orange	1	1	1
Water	4.5 litres	1 gallon	1 gallon
Yeast and nutrient			

Grate the peel from the orange and lemons, avoiding the white pith, and put it in a small muslin bag with the cloves and bruised ginger. Bring the water to the boil, drop in the bag and simmer gently for an hour. Then take out the bag, place the sugar in a polythene bucket, and pour boiling water over it. Stir to dissolve the sugar, and add the yeast nutrient and the juice of the citrus fruits. Allow to cool to 21°C then add the yeast, a wine yeast or one level teaspoonful of granulated yeast. Leave closely covered for four days in a warm place, then stir, pour into fermenting jar, and fit an airlock. Leave till it clears, then siphon off for the first time into fresh jar and refit an airlock. When the wine has cleared completely, has thrown a second deposit, and all fermentation has ceased, bottle.

* ## Cornmeal wine (or 'Golden dynamite')

Ingredients	Metric	British	USA
Yellow cornmeal or cornflour	1 kilo	2 lb	1½ lb
Sugar	1.5 kilos	3 lb	2¼ lb
Lemons, juice	2	2	2
Oranges, juice	3	3	3
Grape juice concentrate	1.75 litres	3 pints	3 pints
Tartaric acid	30 g	1 oz	1 oz
Ammonium phosphate	10 g	¼ oz	¼ oz
Ground rice	10 g	¼ oz	¼ oz
Campden tablets	2	2	2
Water	9 litres	2 gallons	2 gallons
Yeast			

207

November

Mix all the ingredients together, then add yeast (use a good wine yeast) and set aside in a warm place (17–21°C) to ferment, closely covered, for at least 30 days, stirring once a day. Siphon off and 30 days later rack off again; it will then be ready to drink.

* Hop wine

Ingredients	Metric	British	USA
Hops	75 g	3 oz	3 oz
Ginger (bruised)	25 g	1 oz	1 oz
Sugar	1.5 kilos	3 lb	2¼ lb
Orange	1	1	1
Lemon	1	1	1
Water	4.5 litres	1 gallon	1 gallon
Yeast and nutrient			

Boil the hops and ginger in the water for one hour, then strain and pour the liquor over the sugar and orange and lemon juice. Put all into a fermenting jar with wine yeast or a level teaspoonful of granulated yeast, and nutrient, filling only to shoulder, and fit an airlock. When it has fermented nearly out add 250 ml grape concentrate and 225 g (½ lb) of sugar and refit airlock. When no more bubbles pass, bung down tightly. Leave for six months before bottling.

* Parsnip sherry (light)

Ingredients	Metric	British	USA
Young parsnips	2 kilos	4 lb	3 lb
Sugar	1.25 kilos	2½ lb	2 lb
Malt extract	2 tablespoons	2 tablespoons	4 tablespoons
Citric acid	1 teaspoon	1 teaspoon	1 teaspoon
Water	4.5 litres	1 gallon	1 gallon
Yeast and nutrient			
Anti-pectic enzyme			

December

Scrub the parsnips (which are best lifted after the first frost) but do not peel. Cut into chunks or slices and boil gently in the water until tender, then strain. Stir in the malt, acid, pectic enzyme, and sugar, and when cool add the yeast and nutrient. Ferment, closely covered, in a warm place for 10 days, then put into a fermenting bottle and fit an airlock. Siphon it off, and bottle when all fermentation has ceased and wine has cleared.

* Quince wine (dry)

Ingredients	Metric	British	USA
Quinces	20	20	20
Sugar	1.5 kilos	3 lb	2¼ lb
Lemons	2	2	2
Water	4.5 litres	1 gallon	1 gallon
Yeast and nutrient			

Grate the quinces as near to the core as possible, and boil the pulp in the water for 15 minutes (not more, or the wine may not clear subsequently). Strain on to the sugar and add the juice and grated rinds of the two lemons. Allow the liquor to cool before adding the yeast (a wine yeast or a level teaspoonful of granulated yeast) and nutrient. Leave it to stand for 48 hours, closely covered, in a warm place, then strain into fermenting bottle and fit an airlock. Siphon off for the first time when it clears. This wine has a strong individualistic bouquet, but sometimes ferments for an extraordinarily long time, so extra-careful attention to racking is necessary to stabilise it, with the addition of one Campden tablet per gallon finally.

* Sultana sherry (dry)

Ingredients	Metric	British	USA
Sultanas or 'white raisins'	500 g	1 lb	¾ lb
Grapes	500 g	1 lb	¾ lb

December

	Metric	British	USA
Barley	250 g	½ lb	½ lb
Sugar	1.5 kilos	2½ lb	2 lb
Citric acid	½ teaspoon	½ teaspoon	½ teaspoon
Water	4.5 litres	1 gallon	1 gallon
Sherry yeast and nutrient			

Soak the barley overnight in half a pint of (extra) water and the next day mince both grain and sultanas. Bring water to the boil and pour it over the grain and fruit, then crush the grapes manually and add. Stir in the sugar and make sure it is all dissolved. Allow to cool to just tepid, then introduce the nutrient, acid and yeast. Ferment closely covered for 10 days, stirring vigorously daily, then strain into fermenting jar and fit an airlock.

* Spiced beetroot wine (medium)

Ingredients	Metric	British	USA
Beetroot	1.5 kilos	3 lb	2¼ lb
Sugar	1.5 kilos	3 lb	2¼ lb
Cloves	6	6	6
Lemon, juice	1	1	1
Ginger, bruised	25 g	1 oz	1 oz
Water	4.5 litres	1 gallon	1 gallon
Yeast and nutrient			

Wash the beetroot well, but do not peel; cut them up and boil them in some of the water until tender but not mushy. Strain on to the sugar, lemon juice, spices, and the rest of the water, and stir until the sugar is dissolved. When the liquor is cool stir in the yeast, then cover closely, and leave in a warm place, giving it a stir each day. After three days strain the liquor through nylon into an opaque fermenting jar or bottle, and fit an airlock. When it clears siphon it into dark bottles.

It is important that opaque jars or dark bottles should be used, otherwise on exposure to the light beetroot wine will lose the glorious colour which is its principal feature and turn an unattractive brown. If you have only clear glass vessels, wrap them in brown paper, invert sugar bags over them, or keep them in a dark cupboard. Sometimes even these precautions do not work, and it would seem that the colouring pigment in beetroot is decidedly unstable. But if you can retain the colour it is most attractive.

* Ginger wine (dry)

Ingredients	Metric	British	USA
Root ginger	75 g	3 oz	3 oz
Concentrate (white)	280 ml	½ pint	½ pint
Sugar	1.5 kilos	2½ lb	2 lb
Bananas (no skins)	1 kilo	2 lb	1½ lb
Water	4.5 litres	1 gallon	1 gallon
All purpose yeast and nutrient			

Break the root ginger into pieces, and put it and the concentrate into a plastic bucket with the sugar. Pour on 2.5 litres (5 pints) of boiling water. Meanwhile chop the bananas into small pieces and boil them in 500 ml (1 pint) of water until they go mushy, then strain the banana liquid into the bucket, stirring well to dissolve the sugar. Add 1 pint of cold water and, when the mixture is tepid, the yeast and nutrient.

Ferment in a covered bucket for 10 days, stirring twice daily, then strain into a 4.5 litre (1 gallon) jar. Top up to the bottom of neck with cold water. Fit an airlock and leave to ferment. Rack three months later, by then the wine should have stopped fermenting if it has been kept in a warm place. Rack again about three months later. If made this month the wine will be ready for next Christmas – if you manage to keep it that long! Green food colouring purchased from your grocer can be added if one wishes to give some authenticity, then you *will* baffle your friends.

December

* Mixed dried fruit wine

Ingredients	Metric	British	USA
Dried fruit in cartons	1 kilo	3 × 12 oz cartons	2 lb
Wheat	500 g	1 lb	¾ lb
Sugar	1.5 kilos	3 lb	2¼ lb
Citric acid	1 tablespoon	1 tablespoon	2 tablespoons
Water	4.5 litres	1 gallon	1 gallon
Yeast and nutrient			

This is a glorious golden wine which is simplicity itself to make.

Make up a starter bottle two days or so before you need it with half a pint of orange juice – it can be a little diluted to make up the quantity – 30 g (1 oz) of sugar, a little yeast nutrient and the general-purpose wine yeast. Place it in a temperature of about 21°C.

Buy your fruit (sultanas, raisins and currants) cheaply wherever you can. Tip all the fruit, grain and sugar into a bucket, and pour over them the boiling water, stirring to dissolve the sugar. When cool add the contents of the starter bottle and 10 g (¼ oz) citric acid, and stir well in. Cover closely and leave in a warm place 17–21°C for three weeks, stirring vigorously daily. Then strain into fermenting bottle and fit an airlock, and rack off for the first time when it clears. This wine can be drunk after six months and it is doubly useful in that it can be made at any time of the year.

* Parsnip wine (medium)

Ingredients	Metric	British	USA
Parsnips	3 kilos	7 lb	5½ lb
Citric acid	2 tablespoons	2 tablespoons	2 serving spoons
Water	11 litres	2½ gallons	2½ gallons
Sugar	1.5 kilos	3 lb	2½ lb
Yeast and nutrient			
Pectic enzyme			

December

Scrub and scrape the parsnips; then slice them and boil them in the water until tender, *but not mushy, or the wine may not clear later.* The parsnips can be boiled in half the water, if necessary, and the remaining water added afterwards, warm.

Then strain through a coarse cloth tied over a fermenting bin, but do not hurry the process or press the parsnips in any way, for again this may be fatal to the wine's clarity. A thorough, slow, unforced straining is essential. Measure the liquor, add 3 lb white sugar to a gallon, and finally the citric acid. Bring to the boil and simmer for three-quarters of an hour. Turn into bucket, and when liquor has cooled to 21°C add yeast, yeast nutrient and pectic enzyme. Cover closely with a thick cloth and allow to remain in a warm place for ten days, stirring well from the bottom each day. Then strain into fermenting jars, fit airlocks and leave for about six months in a cooler place; it should then be clearing. Siphon it off the lees, bottle, and keep six months longer.

Many people have difficulty in clearing parsnip wine, but if you follow these instructions carefully yours will be of brilliant clarity and excellent colour.

* ## Sarsaparilla wine (medium)

Ingredients	Metric	British	USA
Sarsaparilla	35 g	1½ oz	1½ oz
Caramel	25 g	¾ oz	½ oz
Sugar	1.5 kilos	3 lb	2¼ lb
Tartaric acid	35 g	1½ oz	1 oz
Water	4.5 litres	1 gallon	1 gallon
Yeast and nutrient			

Infuse sarsaparilla and caramel in 1 litre (1½ pints) boiling water, and add sugar. Allow to cool, add 3.5 litres (6½ pints) cold water, acid, nutrient and yeast. Ferment, rack and bottle in usual way.

December

* Wheat wine (sweet)

Ingredients	Metric	British	USA
Wheat	500 g	1 lb	¾ lb
Brown sugar	1.5 kilos	3½ lb	2½ lb
Raisins	1 kilo	2 lb	1½ lb
or Concentrate (white)	560 ml	1 pint	1 pint
Citric acid	2 tablespoons	2 tablespoons	2 serving spoons
Water	4.5 litres	1 gallon	1 gallon
Yeast and nutrient			
Amylozyme			

Soak the wheat in one pint of the water overnight to soften it. Mince the wheat and raisins and then put them or the concentrate in a bowl and pour on hot (not necessarily boiling) water. Add the specified citric acid, and allow to cool to 21°C. Add the enzyme according to supplier's directions, yeast, and yeast nutrient. Cover well with cloth and allow to stand for 10 days, *stirring well daily*. Strain, put into fementing jar, and fit an airlock. Siphon off into bottles when clear and no longer fermenting.

Christleton (by Dr L. W. F. Rowe)

If you, like me, are both mean and lazy, try this recipe! 'Mean and lazy' because it will give you a wine which is both cheap and very easy to make, and drinkable within a couple of months of being started. It's 'a light dry red wine equally suitable for Sunday dinner or for lazing in the garden on a hot sunny day' . . . need I say more?

December/Christmas drinks

Ingredients	Metric	British	USA
Dried elderberries	125 g	4¼ oz	4 oz
Sugar (or glucose)	1 kilo	2 lb	1¾ lb
Dry cider	700 ml	1¼ pints	1¼ pints
Citric acid	2 teaspoons	1 dessertspoon	1 tablespoon
Water	4.5 litres	1 gallon	1 gallon
Wine yeast and nutrient			
Pectolase			
3 × 3 mg Vitamin B tablets			

Place the dried elderberries in a saucepan with enough water to cover them comfortably. Bring to the boil and simmer for 15 minutes. Strain off the juice, pressing lightly, and return the berries to the pan. Add just enough water to cover, bring to the boil again and simmer for 10 minutes. Strain again and repeat this process, simmering for 10 minutes at a time, until just about all the colour has gone out of the berries. Stir the sugar, citric acid and yeast nutrient, into the hot liquid and put aside to cool. When down to about 32°C, add the cider, pectolase and yeast starter (and Vitamin B_1 tablets) and ferment out in the usual way.

Coomassie

In a small tumbler break the yolk of a fresh egg and mix in one teaspoon icing sugar. Add six drops Angostura, 45 ml (1½ oz) sherry and half that amount of brandy. Fill glass with shaved ice, shake well and strain. Dust with fresh grated nutmeg and powdered cinnamon. This approaches a flip.

Advocaat (1)

Whatever you do, do not fail to make this gorgeous advocaat. We can guarantee that this recipe (for which we are indebted to Mr G. Wilson, of Ryde, Isle of Wight) will produce a liqueur of authentic colour and consistency, smooth, creamy and wholly delightful.

December

4 yolks from medium-size eggs
210 ml (7 fl oz) cheap brandy
¾ large tin Ideal milk (the one equivalent to 1¾ pints of milk)
4 oz sugar syrup (2 lb to 1 pint)
1 teaspoon vanilla essence
½ teaspoon saffron yellow food colouring

Put all the ingredients with the exception of the brandy into a liquidiser, and liquidise for 20 seconds. Then pour into the top half of a *double* saucepan with a lid.

Put water in the lower saucepan and boil for about an hour, until the mixture in the upper pan thickens and looks similar to a cooled jelly (when the pan is jerked sideways sharply the mixture will come away from the side and then flop back again). Check that the lower pan does not boil dry.

Leave the mixture to cool, then put into the liquidiser with the brandy for 30 seconds.

If too thick liquidise with some of the remaining Ideal milk. Bottle and leave in a cool place for 24 hours.

Advocaat (2)

Six fresh free range eggs. Whisk the whites with a little sugar and then add yolks. Add 1 tin of *Nestlés* condensed milk and whisk again (tin equivalent to 1⅝ pints fresh milk).

Add 1 pocket size or quarter size brandy and whisk again. Then add about 1¼ pints of wheat or barley wine and whisk again. Taste result. Shake well before drinking.

Angelica liqueur

And here is a recipe for another Christmas luxury:

1 oz angelica stem   1 pint brandy
1 oz boiled bitter almonds   1 pint syrup made with white sugar

Steep the angelica and almonds in the brandy for a week, then strain off and add the syrup to the liquor. Improves with keeping – if you can keep it!

Island magic

. . . and *do* try this superb coffee liqueur by Ren Bellis, of *Making Inexpensive Liqueurs* fame. It hails from the Isle of Islay where, for more than a century, they have been distilling 'the pale golden liquid that wins friends and influences people'.

Take a 2 pint jug and add to it: one 14 oz tin of condensed milk, one 6 oz tin of Ideal milk, one 7 oz carton of long-life single cream, 8 teaspoonfuls (or less, according to taste) of Camp coffee, and 8 oz of whisky. Finally, stir all together and pour.

An earnest Scotch-lover's reaction may be, 'You've ruined some mighty fine Scotch', but a lot of folk will find it wonderful!

Irish cream

. . . and if you like drinks of the Bailey's Irish Cream calibre here is the recipe just for you:

410 g (14.5 oz) can of Carnation milk
383 g (13.5 oz) can of condensed milk
1 teaspoon glycerine
1½ teaspoons T. Noirot extract Cacao
1 breakfast mug of whisky

Tip all the ingredients into a 1-litre bottle, shake well – and sup!

Hot coffee rum

This is another excellent coffee-based after-dinner drink for which, if possible, the coffee should be freshly ground, as well as freshly made.

Into a small saucepan put six lumps of sugar, the finely pared rind of two oranges, six cloves, and a stick of cinnamon. Add enough rum to cover the sugar and bring nearly to the boil, stirring gently until the sugar is dissolved. Take care that it does not catch fire.

When ready stir the mixture into six cups of very strong very hot black coffee and serve immediately.

December/Christmas drinks

Orange cocktail

Mix: 1 bottle orange wine, 1 wineglass whisky, and a dash of rum.

* Christmas glow

1 bottle of one of your red wines	50 g (2 oz) honey
1 small glass cherry brandy	Grated nutmeg to taste
1 glass brandy	About 250 ml (½ pint)
1 sliced lemon	boiling water
1 cup granulated sugar	

Heat wine, honey, lemon, nutmeg, sugar to near boiling point; then add brandy and cherry brandy and lastly the water. Serve immediately.

Christmas punch (white)

For those who like punches (and who doesn't at Christmas?) here is an excellent recipe:

Rub eight pieces of lump sugar on two big lemons, collecting all the fragrant essential oil possible. Put the lumps in a bright saucepan with ¼ teaspoon of ground cinnamon, ¼ teaspoon of grated nutmeg and ground cloves mixed and a fair punch of salt. Put in 250 ml (8 oz) each of brandy and Jamaica rum and add 475 ml (16 oz) of boiling water. Heat up the bowl, and strain into it the juice of two lemons. Heat up the mixture in the pan just to miss boiling point and strain it through muslin in colander or sieve into the bowl. Now add 500 ml (1 pint) of a good white country wine – elderflower, gooseberry, rhubarb or apple, preferably sparkling – and serve with a cube of pineapple in each cup.

* Festive punch (red)

1 bottle elderberry wine	Juice and rind of one lemon
30 g (2 tablespoons) sugar	1 cup of water
3 g (½ teaspoon) mixed spices	6 g (2 oz) raisins
½ cup grapefruit juice	

Heat wine with sugar, spice, and grapefruit juice and lemon rind. Boil the raisins slowly in a cup of water and add to wine mixture. Do not strain. Serve with raisins in a punch bowl.

* Milk punch (modern version of an 1835 recipe)

1 litre (1 quart) fresh milk
1 bottle rum or brandy
500 ml (1 pint) rum (if desired)
4.5 litres (1 gallon) water

6 Seville oranges (or six ordinary oranges and six lemons)
1.5 kilos (3½ lb) sugar

Peel the fruit very thinly, or use a grater to exclude all white pith, which has a bitter taste, and squeeze out all the juice. Soak the peel in the spirits for four days in a corked large bottle. Put the sugar in a bowl and pour on the water, the milk (boiling, if it has not been previously pasteurised) and the fruit juice. Stir well to dissolve the sugar. Strain through a nylon sieve, then bottle. This punch must be drunk within a few days; if you wish to keep it longer than that before serving do not add the water until the last minute, and then add it boiling, since the punch of course should be drunk just warm.

Punch (an old recipe)

Take two or three good fresh lemons, with rough skins quite yellow; some lumps of good sugar; grate a handful of the skins of the lemons, through a bread grater, on to the sugar; then squeeze in the lemons, bruise the sugar and stir the juice well together, for much depends on the process of mixing the sugar and lemons; pour on them 1 litre (1 quart) of boiling water, and again mix them well together (this is called the sherbet); add 570 ml (1½ pints) of brandy, and the same quantity of rum; stir it up, then strain it through a sieve; put in 1 quart (1 litre) of golden or maple syrup, and 1 quart (1 litre) of boiling water.

219

December

Ruby delight

And here is a novelty most home winemakers will be able to compile, and which is very popular with the ladies:

½ bottle blackberry wine	Wineglass ginger wine
½ bottle rhubarb wine	Wineglass port wine
½ wineglass whisky	

* 'Whisky and ginger ale'

15 ml (½ oz) essence ginger	30 g (1 oz) burnt sugar
15 ml (½ oz) essence capsicum	1.2 kilo (2½ lb) brown sugar
10 g (¼ oz) tartaric acid	570 ml (1 pint) white grape
20 drops essence lemon	concentrate
5 drops essence vanilla	5 litres (9 pints) water
Yeast and nutrient	

Buy the first six ingredients from your chemist, grocer or wine supplies shop.

Put the sugar and grape concentrate in bowl and add boiling water, stir to dissolve both, then stir in tartaric acid and lemon essence. When cool add yeast and nutrient, and ferment in the usual way. When fermentation has finished add the ginger, capsicum and vanilla essences.

Do this by degrees, to taste, since the quantities quoted are the maximum. The final step is to carbonate the finished drink in a Ritchie Carbonating Kit or siphon (see page 74) to produce a beverage very similar to a whisky ginger bought over the bar of an average pub.

Winemaking Circles

Winemaking as an organised hobby is a development of the last 40 years, although wines have been made in these islands for centuries in the cottages of country folk. It was only in 1953 that the first "Winemakers' Circle" was formed at Andover, closely followed – quite independently and spontaneously – by others at Welwyn Garden City and Cheltenham. Thereafter, however, the idea spread with astounding speed, and eventually there were over 1,200 such clubs, scattered the length and breadth of the British Isles. There are clubs in Canada and the USA, Zimbabwe, Ireland, Holland, Sweden, Australia and in New Zealand, most of them following the original idea and calling themselves Circles, some of them adopting the style of Guilds, and yet others calling themselves Societies or Associations. The publication of the monthly magazine, *The Amateur Winemaker* (later *Winemaker and Brewer*) from 1958 to 1987 was largely responsible for consolidating the movement and publicising the aims of the Circles.

All of them have the same fundamental objective – the improvement of the standard of country wines – and all of them notably have the same characteristic, a striking friendliness and informality. The Circles are real centres of friendship and good fellowship, as well as means of instruction.

Practical winemaking is learned pleasantly and in a sociable atmosphere by means of talks, demonstrations, quizzes, and competitions, and nowadays there are also inter-club contests. Members learn not only how to make wine, but how to exhibit and judge it.

On the social side, there are usually Christmas or New Year parties, dinners, dances, outings to breweries, sugar refineries, glassworks, potteries, wine lodges, vineyards, and other places of interest to the winemaker.

All in all, members find that joining a Winemakers' Circle is definitely worth while, and anyone interested in the subject would be well advised to contact the nearest one, if they are lucky enough to have one in their area. Send an SAE to *Homebrew Today* (see p. 229 for address for help).

The first National Conference and Show – quite a small affair – was held at Andover in 1959, and others followed at Bournemouth, Brighton, Harrow, Cheltenham, Clacton, Harrogate, Bognor, Torquay, Eastbourne, Nottingham, Scarborough, Margate, Southampton, Llandudno, Blackpool, Weston-super-Mare, and Prestatyn, and the 'National' developed into a mammoth competitive wine show which attracts up to 4800 entries. It is undoubtedly the big event of the year for keen winemakers, and visitors even come from abroad – Germany, Denmark and Canada, for instance.

The show has now grown into the National Association of Winemakers and Brewers (Amateur) and has also led to the formation in 1964 of The Amateur Winemakers' National Guild of Judges (now the National Guild of Wine & Beer Judges, NGWBJ) which set itself the task of getting down on paper a system of wine and beer judging, notes for the guidance of show organisers, judges and judges' stewards, and specimen schedules which clubs or organisations could adopt for their wine competitions.

A tremendous amount of ground work was done on this, and embodied in the handbook which the Guild eventually published, *Judging Home-Made Wines and Beers*, which is periodically revised and updated.

Showing your wines

Eventually, as your stock of wine (and your confidence!) grows your thoughts may turn to entering some of the Circle or open competitions that are run nowadays. Almost every flower and horticultural show has classes for home-made wine and you are not likely to encounter many difficulties so long as you adhere rigidly to any conditions laid down in the schedule *of that particular show.*

Many competitions are run under 'National' rules (as defined by the NGWBJ Judges Handbook), but some shows may have quaint little rules of their own about bottling, labelling and tasting.

So the first thing to do, well in advance of the show date, is to send for a schedule and study it carefully. Next, spend a couple of delightful evenings appraising your own wines and deciding which to enter in the classes you fancy. Here you need to be quite clear on what is dry, what is medium, what is sweet, and on what is expected in classes for each wine type – aperitif, social, dessert, etc. Having decided which classes you might tackle, send in your entry form and fees, if any.

Then get down to preparing your wines. Some may need a final 'polish' or filtering to render them brilliant. Bottles are usually of the Bordeaux type, and they should preferably be of clear white glass, with a 'punt' or conical bottom, which does show off the wine to advantage. But both clear glass and truly punted bottles are now becoming difficult to obtain and judges are now usually prepared to accept the slightly smaller, flatter-punted modern bottle. But it *must* be of the shouldered Bordeaux type, and not the sloping Burgundy or slender Rhine type, or the entry is likely to be ruled 'NAS' ('Not according to Schedule') if the show is being held under 'National' rules.

Your bottles must be scrupulously clean and polished. Fill them to within ¼ to ¾ in. of the bottom of the cork and use a white plastic-topped cork stopper. Stick any label sent you by the entries secretary in the correct place, polish your bottle, and wrap it in tissue against the great day. Deliver it to the show in good time ... and the best of luck!

But how, I can hear you asking, do they actually *judge* wine? And here I run into difficulty, because it is just not possible to describe a taste with pen and paper. And that, of course, is the factor with which one is principally concerned. Taste and knowledge of wine are largely a matter of accumulated comparative experience, and it is up to all winemakers, whether they aspire to judge or not, steadily to increase their knowledge and experience of wine by comparing their own products with those of their fellow members and, indeed, with all types of commercial wine. Only in that way can they acquire the requisite experience, and it is one of the pleasantest aspects of our hobby, as you well know!

A judge will usually assess the wine under five main headings, for which points will be awarded as follows:

Presentation	2
Clarity	4
Colour	4
Bouquet	10
Flavour, balance and quality	30
Total, out of	50

The first two factors will be assessed before opening the bottle.

The judge will look at its general appearance (cleanliness, neatness and legibility of label, size of air space, etc.). Needless to say, the cork must be sound, clean and new, and of the white plastic-topped cork stopper type so that it can be easily drawn and replaced.

The judge will look through the neck of the bottle to judge the clarity of the wine, and at the conical 'punt' at the bottom to judge its brilliance. Here there should not be the slightest trace of any yeast or other deposit. A star-bright wine will score points over a bright, or a merely clear, wine. Wise exhibitors bottle their wine for show several days ahead after having made sure that it has been adequately racked, therefore minimising the risk of having any yeast deposit.

A little of the wine is then poured into a glass, and checked for colour, which should be clear and appropriate, and for the bouquet, which must be enticing, making one want to taste the wine; it must be vinous, 223 pleasing, and well developed, but not overpoweringly so.

But, when all is said and done, it is the taste of the wine which naturally carries the most marks. The flavour of a wine must be agreeable, reasonably redolent of the fruit or source of origin (though not so much as some expect), vinous and invigorating, with sufficient 'bite', enough acid, adequate strength for its purpose (i.e. aperitif, table or dessert) and the correct degree of dryness or sweetness. It should, above all, be well balanced as between sweetness, acidity and astringency, and be free of bacterial or other faults.

Between tastes the judge will clear his or her palate with biscuit, bread, or fresh water.

Judging procedure is set out in detail in the Guild of Judges Handbook and wine clubs will find it fascinating to study these clear directions and arrange competitions to give their members judging practice. This can be done by having, say, up to 10 bottles of wine available and giving each member a judging sheet on which are set out the possible points to be scored under each heading.

Organising a wine competition

If, however, you are a club secretary or official, or even are known locally as someone who 'knows a bit about wine', you are liable suddenly to find yourself faced with a request by some flower show or other to lay down rules and regulations for a wine class which the committee is thinking of including for the first time.

Your first action should be to study the Judges' Guild Handbook, *Judging Home-Made Wines and Beers*, carefully.

Secondly, you have to decide how many, and what, classes you can have (or afford) on this occasion. You should bear in mind that a single wine class is not much use, for no judge can really judge a sweet wine side by side with a dry. Once he has tasted a really sweet wine his palate for drier wines is destroyed for that day! At least two classes are therefore desirable, and more if possible. Probably the minimum is four: Red, dry and sweet, and White, dry and sweet, but many Circles prefer having medium categories as well, so that one then has dry, medium and sweet (white and red = six classes). It is not really possible to define these in terms of specific gravity; the best one can do is to say that a really dry wine is likely to be below 1000.

Given these three main classifications it is an age-old argument as to how wines should be further broken down into small numbers desirable

A National Association of Wine and Beer Makers Annual Show, held at Nottingham University.

for a class. Should they be described by ingredient, e.g. 'Parsnip, sweet', 'Redcurrant, dry', or by purpose, e.g. 'Red table wine, dry', 'Dessert wine, white'? There are two schools of thought, and it is for you to decide which you prefer.

Where there are only, say, four classes, golden and tawny wines will have to go in with the white, and rosé wines with the reds, but it is much better if they can be in separate classes.

Having decided upon your classes, you can proceed to draw up some rules. You can short-circuit this by simply adopting the Guild of Judges standard set of rules, but here are some of the points which you must obviously cover; others may well occur in individual cases.

Rules

Standard 75 cl (26⅔ fl oz) bottles and no half-bottles should be used, and they should be of clear or at worst lightly tinted glass. (Even red wines should be shown in clear bottles, so that the presentation and clarity can be judged.)

225

All bottles should be of the Bordeaux shape (not Burgundy, Hock or any other variety) and should preferably have a 'punt', or concave bottom, whether deep or shallow.

The airspace should be between ¼ in. and ¾ in.

No separate small tasting bottle (to avoid the necessity of opening the bottle exhibited) should be allowed, and exhibitors should be told that the actual bottle will be opened and tasted.

Bottles should be securely corked, preferably with a stopper cork, which may be wired for travelling, but the wires or ties must be removed before benching.

Labels should preferably be supplied by the organisers, and be about 2 in. by ¾ in., so fixed that the bottom edge of the label is an inch above the bottom of the bottle. On the labels should appear only the description of the wine, by use or ingredient according to the type of schedule adopted.

Judges

How many judges?

This is a difficult decision unless you can estimate how many entries you are likely to get, but it is generally agreed that 40 bottles is a reasonable stint for any judge, which he should be able to do in a couple of hours.

More than that, his palate becomes jaded and he becomes loquacious! Talking of preserving palates, see to it that some provision is made of a palate cleaner; bread or dry biscuits are popular, while some judges use plain water. Supply the judge, too, with reasonable working space and a bucket of water for rinsing glasses. Other equipment he should bring.

Preferably appoint a steward to assist each judge, and introduce them to one another at a pre-judging briefing, which will give you a chance to hand out working sheets, award cards, and other paper work, and explain any particular points.

Appoint other stewards to receive the entries at the fixed hour, and a reliable mathematician as scorer and recorder, and you're in business.

Appendix A

The following conversion tables give exact equivalents.

Weight

British to Metric

	5 lb	=	2.267 kilogrammes
	4 lb	=	1.814 kilos
	3 lb	=	1.360 kilos
	2 lb	=	907 grammes
	1 lb	=	453 g
	½ lb	=	226 g
	¼ lb	=	113 g
	1 oz	=	30 g (approx.)
Tablespoon	½ oz	=	15 g (approx.)
Dessertspoon	¼ oz	=	10 g (approx.)
Teaspoon	⅛ oz	=	5 g (approx.)

Metric to British

5 kilogrammes	=	11 lb
4 kilos	=	8 lb 12 oz
3 kilos	=	6 lb 9 oz
2 kilos	=	4 lb 6 oz
1 kilo	=	2 lb 3 oz
500 grammes	=	1 lb 1½ oz
250 g	=	8¾ oz
125 g	=	4½ oz
100 g	=	3½ oz
50 g	=	1½ oz

Capacity

British to Metric

	1 gallon	=	4.546 litres
		=	4546 millilitres (or ccs)
	1 pint	=	568 ml/cc
	½ pint	=	284 ml/cc
	1 fl oz	=	28 ml/cc
Tablespoon	½ fl oz	=	15 ml/cc
Dessertspoon	¼ fl oz	=	10 ml/cc
Teaspoon	⅛ fl oz	=	5 ml/cc

Metric to British

5 litres	=	8 pints 14 oz
4½ litres	=	7 pints 18 oz
4 litres	=	7 pints
3 litres	=	5 pints 5 oz
2 litres	=	3 pints 10 oz
1 litre	=	1 pint 14 oz
500 millilitres	=	17 oz
250 ml/cc	=	8½ oz
125 ml/cc	=	4¼ oz
100 ml/cc	=	3½ oz
50 ml/cc	=	1¾ oz

To convert	*into*	*Multiply by*
Cubic centimetres or millilitres	Fluid ounces	.036
Fahrenheit	Centigrade	Subtract 32, multiply by 5, divide by 9
Centigrade	Fahrenheit	Multiply by 9, divide by 5, and add 32

Appendix B

Some useful addresses:

Send 2 × 26p stamps for a sample copy of *Homebrew Today* to:
The Editor, *Homebrew Today*
304 Northridge Way
Hemel Hempstead
Herts. HP1 2AB

For a catalogue of new & second-hand wine & beermaking books, 2 × 25p
stamps to:
Brewbooks
4 Lytles Close
Formby
Liverpool L37 4BT

For a copy of the Judges' Handbook, contact:
NGWBJ Supplies Officer:
Mr. J. Keeley
15 Crescent Ave.
Over Hulton
Bolton
Lancs. BL5 1EN

For information about NAWB write to:
The Membership Secretary
National Assoc. of Wine & Beermakers
Mrs J. Dinnage
22 Golden Hind Park
Dibden Purlieu
Southampton
Hants. SO4 5BN

Index

232

234

236

Also available from Nexus Special Interests

130 NEW WINEMAKING RECIPES (C. J. J. BERRY)
Contains tested and reliable recipes, many of which are unique to this publication, but certain well-tried favourites are also included.

MAKING WINES LIKE THOSE YOU BUY
(BRYAN ACTON and PETER DUNCAN)
How to reproduce the flavour and quality of commercial wines in your own home. Sauternes, hocks, Madeiras and champagne are all possibilities with the help of this book.

MAKING SPARKLING WINES (J. RESTALL and D. HEBBS)
The authors have spent decades exploring the techniques of sparkling wine production, and in discovering the secrets of producing champagne-like wine of superb quality. In this revised and updated edition they share their expertise – whether you are a beginner or an experienced winemaker, you will find this book contains all the information necessary to make your own sparkling wines.

WINEMAKING WITH CONCENTRATES (PETER DUNCAN)
Reprinted in its original form, here at last is a book for the winemaker who likes the ease and convenience of making wine from concentrates. The recipes are formulated from concentrates which are readily available. This is the book every winemaker who uses concentrates will want in his library for ready reference.

HOME BREWED BEERS AND STOUTS (C. J. J. BERRY)
The first modern book on home brewing, this was an instant success when it was first published in 1963. This latest edition contains up-to-date information on how to brew fine beers and stouts of authentic flavours and strength.

BREWING BEERS LIKE THOSE YOU BUY (DAVID LINE)
Contains full instructions for making real draught ale, bottled and keg beers, lagers and stouts from over one hundred recipes collected from around the world, all at a fraction of pub prices.

All the above titles are available from good bookshops. In case of difficulty contact Nexus Special Interests, Nexus House, Boundary Way, Hemel Hempstead, Herts HP2 7ST Tel: 01442 66551.